GIRL, THERE'S A CHAMPION IN YOU FEATURING AUTHOR ANGEL EWINGS

GIRL, THERE'S A CHAMPION IN YOU
FEATURING AUTHOR ANGEL EWINGS

Copyright © 2025 by
All rights reserved. No part of this book may be reproduced in any manner whatsoever without written permission except in the case of brief quotations embodied in critical articles and reviews.
First Printing, 2025

Dedication

For the champions who showed me how to stand in my power before I knew what power was...

To my late grandmother, Constance Elaine Hallman, whose spirit guides me still. You planted the seeds of faith in my soul and whispered, "You are made for greatness," long before I could see it in myself. Your unwavering belief became the foundation upon which I built my courage, and your wisdom echoes in every decision I make.

To my late grandfather, Roosevelt Hallman, whose legacy lives on in every challenge I face. You stepped into the role of father with quiet dignity and fierce love. You taught me that excellence isn't optional and that studying is a sacred discipline. The entrepreneurial fire you kindled continues to light my path, and I feel your strength whenever I stand in my power.

To my mother, Minnie Williams, my quiet coach who never clipped my wings even when my dreams seemed too vast. You have steadied me through every storm and celebrated every victory as if it were your own.

To my beautiful cousin Carmen Campbell, who supported me and believed in me every step of the way. You have not only shown me with your words of encouragement, but you backed it up with your actions. Words cannot speak to what you have done for me. Thank you for giving me a lifeline when I was on what I thought was my eighth life—some of us really do have nine lives. I love you, and I will be there for you always.

VI - DEDICATION

To my daughter, Kierra A. Moore, whom I love with all my heart and who has thrown me a lifeline on more than one occasion. Everything I do, I do for you to show you that the impossible is possible, to show you how to be a champion fighter and how to fight with ease. To know that if you prepare for the fight, you may get hit in the fight, but resilience and discipline will surely bring you the TKO in life. You are the future I fight for, the legacy that drives me to excellence. May this work show you what's possible when you refuse to dim your light.

To my boxing coach, J. R. McKinney, thank you for teaching me that champions aren't born in victory but forged in resilience. The boxing ring became my classroom, and the lessons I learned extended far beyond the physical fight.

And to my husband, Wesley, I thank you for your quiet love that speaks volumes. For the countless late nights you supported without complaint, for the space you've given me to grow into myself, and for loving the woman I am becoming just as much as the woman I've been. I love you for allowing me to be authentically, unapologetically me.

This book is for every Black woman who has ever been told to wait her turn, to dream smaller, to take up less space. Your champion is waiting.

It's time to let her rise.

Foreword

When my daughter Mary first told me about her anthology project, I must admit—I ran straight to the dictionary! Once I understood what an anthology truly was, I was all in. I've always been Mary's most realistic and loudest cheerleader, but this collection of stories from Black women about their journeys? This is something that's going to set the world on fire.

As a Black woman who came up in the business world working for Fortune 500 companies like American Express and Sprint, I know firsthand how hard it was—hard for women in general, but harder for Black women. We had the courage, we had the brains, we had it all, but we were still fighting just to get our foot in the door.

That's why these stories matter so much: because we are still fighting, and because when you are having a hard time, you can't see that there is somebody just like you having a hard time too.

I see Mary's champion spirit shining through this project, just as it did when she was deep into cheerleading as a young girl. I remember how she would go out and raise money for their cheerleading camps—she wouldn't ask me for the money; she would sell candy apples. I also see Mary's champion spirit as she climbed the corporate ladder.

I recall she had her first Black male leader, and she was so happy, although she was still one of few Blacks in the group. She was working so hard for him, trying to help him and the group, and the harder she worked, the more difficult he became to work for because of his own insecurities and lack of knowledge.

But Mary was working night and day trying to help him, help the team. She didn't give up and continued to do her best, and in the end, she was the only one left standing.

I was a single mother with three kids, and early in my career, I always worked two or three jobs. It took two jobs to make a decent salary, and the third job was something extra just in case something happened with the kids.

It's not like we would have been homeless or anything, but I was determined to provide the best for my children, and they wanted for nothing. I never gave up and ended up working for Fortune 500 companies like American Express and Sprint.

Mary's journey has taught me something powerful—that regardless of age or your knowledge base, you can always do what you really want to do. You just need to step up and step out. I learned this lesson from my own parents, who raised six of us, with Mary's grandparents being significant figures in her life, especially as mentioned in Chapter 1.

As the oldest of my siblings, I carried that responsibility just as Mary does now, as the oldest of my three children.

When I faced my own breaking points, those moments when I couldn't take another step and thought to myself, "I cannot do this,". But somehow, I found the strength to continue. That's why "The Breaking Point" chapter resonated with me so deeply. We all face these moments, but it's what we do next that defines us.

To every woman reading these pages: there truly is a champion in you. Sometimes you just need to be reminded of your power, your resilience, and your worth. This anthology is that reminder.

These stories—including my daughter's—are testaments to the strength that lies within all of us, often hidden but never extinguished. With pride and belief in your journey,

Your mom and corner coach,

Minnie Williams

Prologue

THE GARDEN BEGINS—WELCOME TO THE CHAMPION'S JOURNEY
By Mary H. Davis

"Every champion was once a seed planted in fertile ground, watered by dreams, and nurtured by those who came before."

A Movement Begins Here

In the tradition of our ancestors who planted seeds of hope in impossible soil, who grew gardens in concrete, who made feasts from scraps, this book is more than an anthology—it is a declaration. A rising tide. A testament to the strength, wisdom, and resilience of Black women who dare to step into their power.

Like the gardens our grandmothers tended—from backyard plots that fed whole neighborhoods to windowsill herbs that seasoned our food and healed our bodies—our stories have been cultivated with care. Each chapter in this book represents a seed planted—one that will blossom into legacy, impact, and transformation for generations to come.

And as Galatians 6:9 reminds us: 'Let us not grow weary in doing good, for at the proper time we will reap a harvest if we do not give up.' These stories are proof that the harvest is near.

Voices of Our Garden

The women who have shared their voices here are **keepers of our legacy**, telling stories that echo the strength of Harriet, the wisdom of Maya, the fire of Fannie Lou, and the grace of Dorothy Height. From A. Ewings rising from the ashes, to T. Elliott's call to R.O.A.R, to T. Boswell's revelations of freedom—these sisters have unearthed the truth within themselves so that we might all stand taller.

Their stories remind us that no champion rises alone.

Garden Truth: "When we harvest wisdom together, the feast feeds generations."

What You'll Discover in These Pages

- **Resilience:** How we reclaim our voices, no matter what storms we've endured. Like the mighty baobab tree, our roots run deep and our branches reach toward tomorrow's sky.
- **Power:** The unshakable confidence to build, lead, and create new paths. We are the daughters of queens and warriors, entrepreneurs and educators, healers and hope-bearers.
- **Sisterhood:** The bonds that make us stronger together. In the tradition of our sacred circles, kitchen table councils, and sister-friend connections that sustain us through every season.

Each chapter is a thread in the rich fabric of Black womanhood—woven with struggle, triumph, and an unrelenting pursuit of purpose. We are the pattern-makers, the culture-shapers, the dream-defenders.

The Champion's Journey is Just Beginning

This is only the beginning. **These pages are not the final chapter of our journey** but the fertile ground for what comes next. Like the gardens of our ancestors that fed communities and fueled revolutions, these stories are seeds of liberation—nurtured by our voices, strengthened by our struggles, and destined to bloom into a legacy that will nourish generations to come.

With every page you turn, every lesson you absorb, and every truth you embrace, you become part of this ever-growing garden of champions. And while this volume captures the voices of today, **our future is limitless.**

The next generation of champions is watching, learning, and waiting for us to clear the path. Their stories—perhaps yours—will take root in what we build together. As our foremothers taught us: 'Lift as you climb, for no sister should rise alone.

Your Invitation to Grow

"As we stand on the shoulders of those who came before us, we commit to lifting others as we rise."

This book is your plot in our collective garden. These stories are your seeds. Your experiences—the struggles, the victories, the wisdom passed down—are the rich soil that will nourish new growth. Every triumph shared here is water for your roots. Every lesson learned is sunshine for your spirit.

And as Isaiah 61:3 declares, we are 'oaks of righteousness, a planting of the Lord for the display of His splendor.' You were planted with purpose, and this is your season to rise.

The seeds have been planted. The soil is fertile. The season is right.

Are you ready to grow?

"For every Black woman who has ever been told her dreams were too big, her voice too loud, her hair too bold, her ambitions too high—this garden grows for you."

Contents

Dedication — v
Foreword — vii
Prologue — xi

Angel Ewings — 3
  1 THE PHOENIX PROCESS — 4
Mary H. Davis — 14
  2 UNLEASHING YOUR INNER CHAMPION — 15
Tivona Elliott — 31
  3 MEMOIR OF A MISFIT — 32
Tinesha Boswell — 48
  4 F.R.E.E. — 49
Tamara Rivers — 62
  5 THE FALL-THE VOID-THE RISE — 63
Monique Howell — 72
  6 UNCHAINED — 73
Porsha Vidaurre — 83
  7 TENDER HEARTS, STRONG SPIRITS — 84
Marsha Ford — 93
  8 DROPPING JEWELS — 94
Cynthia Holmes — 103

9	BRUISED BUT BRAVE	104
	Joyce Smith-Reid	114
10	THREADS OF TRIUMPH	115
	April L. Jacobs	125
11	UNQUENCHABLE SPIRIT	126
	Angel Diggs	137
12	RISE AND SHINE	138
	Michelle Warren	145
13	BINDING THE BROKEN VOWS	147
	Kenya Cobb-Myers	157
14	WIFE, WORKER, WONDER WOMAN	158
	Verna Lee Burney	171
15	INTRINSIC HAPPINESS	172
	Monica Alexander	178
16	BREAKING BOUNDARIES	179
	Thelesa Moore	189
17	SAVVY SINGLE SISTER	190
	Mary H. Davis	200
18	THE FINAL ROUND	201

About the Curator   209

Angel Ewings

THE PHOENIX PROCESS
Rising From the Ashes of Adversity

1

THE PHOENIX PROCESS

RISING FROM THE ASHES OF ADVERSITY
By: Angel Ewings

Angel Ewings, founder of Wings of an Angel, is mentoring and consulting. It's hard to fly when your wings are injured and weighed down; that's why I'm here to extend mine. With my faith anchored in God, coupled with an optimistic and resilient mindset.

Empowered to overcome life obstacles physically and spiritually, breaking generational traumas, as I journey to be the highest version of myself. Just like the Phoenix, once you go through the fire you emerge stronger, brighter to soar to unlimited heights. Connect with Angel @AngelHunniDew on Facebook.com

Principle: Faith fuels my resilience, guiding me to break free from toxic ties and habits, embrace change despite fear, and discover my true purpose, even when the path is unclear.

Listen up, sisters. We're about to get real. This ain't no sugar-coated fairy tale or some rosy feel-good story. This is about the nitty-gritty of rising from the ashes when life's done burned you down. It's about that unbreakable spirit that's been passed down to us through generations of strong Black women.

I'm Angel Ewings, and I'm here to tell you that your pain isn't just pain – it's the fuel for your rebirth. We're talking about a faith that's not just Sunday morning pretty, but Monday morning gritty. A faith that gets its hands dirty in the trenches of life and comes out shining like gold.

So buckle up, sis. We're about to take a journey through the fire, and I promise you, we're gonna come out on the other side not just surviving, but thriving.

My Lowest Place: Made the Best Leaping Pad

Let me paint you a picture of rock bottom. Imagine a young Black girl, barely out of her teens, standing at the graveside of both her mother figures. The weight of grief presses down so hard it feels like you can't breathe. That was me at 19, feeling like the world had just sucker-punched me and stolen my air.

I was raised in a multi-generational household, so most of my foundational beliefs were from my grandmother, Ruby. Losing her at the age of sixteen was heartbreaking; I had experienced some deaths, but never endured a loss so close. I had lost a major pillar in my world, but had no idea of the impact her absence would have on me or my family.

We all can attest that when Grandma/Big Mama passes away, the family dynamics are never the same. With my mother being the eldest girl and living in the family home with my grandfather, she stepped into the matriarchal shoes.

We went through a strained time of mother-teenager issues, but once I became pregnant at eighteen, we strengthened our bond. Never would I have imagined that my mother watching me graduate from high school and witnessing my first child be born would be the last milestones that we shared together.

The breaking I felt from the death of my mother, Gail, numbed me and paralyzed my mental perception. It sent me in a downward spiral of drinking, partying, and sexing just so I could feel. With another major pillar lost, I was just going through the motions.

But here's the thing about being at the bottom – there's nowhere to go but up. And sometimes, when you're flat on your back, you get the clearest view of the stars.

Affirmation: *"I am the daughter of queens and warriors. Their strength flows in my veins, and their wisdom guides my steps."*

Sisters, when you're in that low place, remember this: it's not your final destination. It's your launching pad. Every tear you cry is watering the seeds of your future greatness.

Opportunity for Change: When My Mind & Heart Aligned

Now, let me tell you about the moment everything shifted. It was October 2020, right in the thick of COVID. The world was in chaos, but inside me, something was aligning. But deep in my soul, there was this pull – a call to something greater.

I was feeling stagnant, unfulfilled, and trapped in toxic relationships. Trying to repair and make amends with my adult daughter. Overcompensating for my guilt of where I felt I failed as a parent. Accepting disrespectful boundaries, I thought never would.

Then there was the lack of self-esteem and codependency I struggled with; I had the hardest time cutting ties with my drug-addicted ex-husband. I love him most definitely, but not at the expense of continuing to devalue myself for over-stimulated orgasm.

I hated my passive-aggressive way of always feeling like I had to give so much or show up for people all the time, even when I felt depleted and unappreciated. I no longer recognized myself and who I had become, what I was tolerating. My days were filled with anxiety and uncertainty.

Group therapy had me open up, unleash some baggage. I realized that before I could help anyone, I had to get real with me and heal these suppressed and bleeding traumas.

I needed to get away, so I went to visit a sister-friend in Georgia for my 45th birthday in June.

On my second day there, I had this overwhelming feeling that this is where I am supposed to be. It felt like I was at home. The radiant warmth and glow of the sun, the peacefulness of the green land, and the openness welcomed me in. I went to get a change of fresh air and scenery, and I got the calling and direction I needed.

Sisters, when your mind and heart align, magic happens. It's like the universe conspires to make things fall into place. But let me be clear – this ain't about waiting for a sign. It's about being brave enough to make the sign yourself.

I said I was going to build an empire, leave a legacy. Why? One thing I knew for sure, through all my years of serving in church and my personal relationship with God, was that what I was called to do was bigger than just me. It was for my lineage.

Affirmation: "I am the architect of my destiny. My mind and heart are aligned, guiding me towards my divine purpose."

Remember this: Holding on to what no longer serves you will keep you delayed from what God has for you. It's time to let go and grow.

Following the Calling: Even When I Didn't Understand the Direction

Let me tell you, following your calling ain't always about having a clear GPS signal from God. Sometimes, it's about taking that first step even when the path ahead is foggy as hell.

When I decided to move to Atlanta, I didn't have all the answers. What I had was faith – a faith that burned brighter than my fears. I had spiritual after-life encounters with my loved ones, heavy concern for my family, and a deep understanding that there are no coincidences when it comes to generational concerns.

My decision to make this major life-changing decision to leave all I've ever known, I needed to receive a clear sign, cause sometimes I can be hasty. I sought a medium (someone who channels messages from the afterlife), seeing that all my wise elders had passed away.

The medium was frigid on her right side and asked, "How did your mother pass away?" I answered acknowledging an aneurysm. My mother instantly channeled through and said, "I am ready to go home. She doesn't like where I'm at, and there's no room for her.

She reaffirmed she knows that I'm not from Georgia, but it's as if I left something unfinished there. I did live in GA no more than a year tops.. twice when I was eleven and when I was thirteen. She went on to ask me if a little girl had passed away around the age of twelve. Bewildered, I answered No! This is when my father came through. My dad passed away when I was 32.

Milton apologized to me for not being there to protect me when I was a child. He then placed the twelve-year-old's hand in my 45-year-old hand and let her know I would take care of her. Through group therapy, I learned that when you experience some traumas or loss, it can cause a separation or interruption in you. She revealed to me that we just experienced a soul reconnection.

Sisters, your calling might not come as a burning bush or a voice from the heavens. It might be that persistent tug on your heart, that idea that won't let you sleep at night. Don't ignore it.

Remember what Harriet Tubman said: "Every great dream begins with a dreamer. Always remember, you have within you the strength, the patience, and the passion to reach for the stars to change the world."

Affirmation: "I trust the journey, even when I don't understand the destination. My faith guides me, and my purpose propels me forward."

Transformation Took Place in Isolation

Now, let's talk about the beauty of isolation. In a world that's always buzzing, always connected, sometimes the most profound changes happen when we're alone with ourselves.

For me, that isolation came with my move to Atlanta. Away from the familiar, away from the noise, I found myself face to face with... myself. And let me tell you, it wasn't always pretty.

It took me four months to secure a corporate job and eight months to sign the lease to my very own Loft townhome-style apartment in Stone Mountain, GA.

I'm forever grateful for the few frienmailies (friends like family) that supported and assisted me once I got to Georgia. I mean, let's be real, although I was blazing my own trail; NONE of us gets through life without some assistance. The universe has always aligned the needed sources at the right time.

Instinctively, I was programmed to seek out male interaction, but knowing I didn't have the emotional or mental capacity to give to someone. Any attempts have been shut down, and the spirit kept reminding me. "You didn't come down here for this.", "Stay focused"! This was the second transformation; the first was being away from my family. This was the first time since being a teen that I truly had to rest in my singleness.

Sexual strongholds were the biggest signature of trauma pain I've carried and needed to be delivered from. I discovered that what I thought was something I controlled was really a toxic, manipulated form of control that was holding me in bondage.

In that solitude, I had to get real honest with myself. I had to face the ugly parts, the wounded parts, the dishonest parts. I had to confront the ways I'd been people-pleasing, the ways I'd been silencing my own voice.

Sisters, this is where the real work happens. In the quiet moments when it's just you and your truth. It's where you strip away the layers of who you thought you should be and discover who you really are.

Affirmation: "In solitude, I find my strength. In silence, I hear my truth. In isolation, I forge my future."

Discovering Who I Am While Identifying My Purpose

Now we're getting to the good part. The part where all that pain, all that growth, all that soul-searching starts to come together like pieces of a divine puzzle.

Discovering who you are isn't a destination – it's a journey. And let me tell you, it's the most rewarding journey you'll ever take. For me, it meant diving deep into my spirituality, exploring plant-based healing, and reconnecting with the ancestral wisdom that runs in our veins.

Even with praying, reading the Bible, and sermons, through my praise and worship, it was a disconnect. I was getting answers and direction.

I just didn't know how the change was going to come. Late-night social media strolls I came across the healing modality of psilocybin plant medicine journeys.

Last year I had my first experience with my Shaman Vizion. My intentions were to discover my purpose and break generational curses. Deliverance of my sexual traumas was only one of the life-transforming encounters I have healed.

I got confirmation of my purpose. Not only to tell my story but use my voice to break free and heal the curses that have plagued my ancestral lineage. Many have been called, few are chosen, but are you willing to take the charge? I accept and so it begins.

Sisters, your purpose isn't something you find – it's something you uncover. It's been there all along, waiting for you to be ready to see it.

As Zora Neale Hurston said, "There are years that ask questions and years that answer." This is your time for answers. This is your time to shine.

Affirmation: "I am discovering my authentic self and embracing my divine purpose. My life is a testament to the power of transformation and self-love."

The Phoenix Rises

We've been through the fire, sisters. We've felt the heat, we've been reduced to ashes, but look at us now – rising, glowing, ready to set the world ablaze with our light.

Remember this: You are worthy of whatever sacrifice it takes to become the highest version of yourself.

Your journey of transformation isn't just for you – it's for every Black woman who will look at you and see what's possible.

You are the phoenix. You are the dream and the dreamer. You are the legacy of every strong Black woman who came before you, and you're paving the way for every Black girl who will come after.

Affirmation: "I am resilient. I am powerful. I am a phoenix rising from the ashes, ready to illuminate the world with my purpose and passion."

Reflections and Takeaways

Innerstand - your healing/self-discovery journey is not about changing locations physically, but it requires a paradigm-shifting of your mindset and actions.

You can not run from you! There are plenty of resources to help you, but no one is coming to save you.

You have free will and power to change yourself and your situation. Don't fret about the task you have to save yourself.

Not only are you equipped for the task... you're the only one that's qualified to become the best version of you. What is it going to take?

- God/Source is the change agent
- Your Faith/belief empowered with prayer and good intentions, is the catalyst that brings it into fruition
- Commitment and dedication you put into yourself will be a sacrifice, but necessary
- Above all else, know that you matter! You are worth fighting for!
- Never give up on YOU – Spread your Wings and Let's Soar Sis

As we close this chapter on rising from the ashes, we open the door to new possibilities. In the next chapter, we'll explore how to harness this newfound strength and purpose to create the life you've always dreamed of. Remember, sister, your transformation doesn't end here – it's only just beginning. The phoenix has risen. Now, it's time to reign.

Mary H. Davis

UNLEASHING YOUR INNER CHAMPION
THE POWER OF RESILIENCE AND AUTHENTICITY

2

UNLEASHING YOUR INNER CHAMPION

THE POWER OF RESILIENCE AND AUTHENTICITY

By Mary H. Davis

"Power is not given to you. You have to take it." – Beyoncé

Standing in your authentic power requires no permission—your excellence and expertise speak for themselves.

The Champion's Call

My Champion Sisters, before we dive in, let's get one thing clear: This anthology isn't just about reading—it's about rising.

Every word here is a seed, every story a root, every lesson a branch reaching toward your greatness. As you read, don't just absorb—activate. Your transformation begins now.

I. The Awakening: A Moment of Truth

The Breaking Point

It was the early 2000s, a time of aggressive bank mergers as financial institutions expanded their national reach. The CEO of the bank I worked for had made it clear—our institution would be one of the last banks standing. Growth through mergers and acquisitions was the strategy, and by then, I had already been part of over 300 successful mergers and acquisitions.

But with this rapid expansion came serious problems. One of the most pressing? The bank's information security framework was a disaster waiting to happen.

Regulatory bodies were watching, compliance issues were stacking up, and the unresolved security risks were threatening the entire M&A strategy.

And then there was me.

A young Black woman, a single mother, in her early 30s, was assigned as special project lead to fix the mess.

Let me be clear—this was a high-stakes mission. My career was starting to take off fast.

- If I succeeded, I would prove myself to be an undeniable asset to the organization.
- If I failed, I would likely be displaced, blackballed, and discarded.

And let's talk about the team I was leading—a room full of white men, all in their late 40s and 50s, each with 20+ years in IT and cybersecurity. The moment I walked in, I saw the unspoken question in their eyes:

"What the hell is she doing here?"

They understood the technical landscape—mainframes, cyber threats, IT protocols. But they didn't know compliance. They didn't know regulatory risk. They didn't know how to create an integrated security strategy to keep the bank's billion-dollar mergers from crumbling under scrutiny.

That's why I was in the room.

So, I did what I always did—I studied relentlessly. I absorbed everything about IT security, read and studied white papers, interviewed leaders and subject matter experts, dissected policies, triple-checked every note and risk factor. I came prepared.

And yet, when the time came to present my findings, these men did what they always do.

They regurgitated my work as if they had discovered it themselves. It was like I was invisible.

I sat there, watching them flex their technical expertise, throwing out bits and pieces of the very issues I had uncovered, parroting the exact solutions I had discussed with them in private—solutions they had pushed back against just days before.

My heart raced. My jaw clenched.

Look at these MFs.

For a split second, the rage boiled over.

I wanted to say it straight:

"Shut the fuck up with your lying ass. You gave me hell when I first brought these issues to you."

But then—I heard my grandmother's voice in my head:

"Mary, you come from greatness, and you have a great biblical name. You were divinely designed for greatness. You can do anything He puts in your path."

Then my grandfather's wisdom followed:

"They can only limit you and steal from you if you let them. Be knowledgeable. Be confident. And be skilled in your communication."

In that moment, I had a choice—react emotionally or move strategically.

So, I sat up straight, let the silence build, and then I spoke.

"I met with each of you last week to discuss these potential issues," I began, my voice clear and unwavering.

Then I repeated their own words back to them—the exact objections they had raised when I first presented the findings.

"I'm glad to see my initial assessments resonated with you."

I detailed every meeting, every challenge, every concern they had dismissed—and as I spoke, the room fell silent.

Faces flushed.

Eyes darted around the table.

The senior leader who appointed me raised an eyebrow.

And then, the subtle nod—my validation.

I had arrived.

I was done playing small.

Reflection: When was the last time you let someone take credit for your work? How did it make you feel? What would you do differently if you could reclaim that moment?

Say it with me—I am done playing small. Say it again—I am worthy of every blessing that's coming to me. One more time—I was born to shift the atmosphere.

Because the moment you believe that? Everything changes.

II. The Transformation: Rising Above Risk

"I didn't wait for a door to open—I built my own. I didn't ask for a seat—I claimed the whole table. When you stop waiting for permission, you step fully into your power." – Mary H. Davis

Let me tell you about the moment I stopped asking for permission to lead and started taking up space like I was born to.

It was 2016, and I had just completed 15+ years in risk management.

My track record spoke for itself:

Led the implementation of three major risk frameworks

- Saved the company millions in regulatory fines.
- Served as a risk and control expert, helping win multi-million-dollar litigation
- Built a reputation as the go-to expert for complex risk and compliance issues

When our Executive of Risk & Controls confided in me that she would need to do a reorganization to align with the enterprise's new risk initiatives and framework, I knew this was my moment. The role seemed tailor-made for my expertise—overseeing risk assessments, which included regulatory compliance, and developing enterprise-wide risk mitigation strategies for over 5,000 branches that had interdependencies with over 100 business products and functional business units.

This should have been a straightforward promotion. I was already doing the job, I provided the criteria for the job, which matched my background perfectly, and I provided the framework for how the organization should be restructured for peak performance. Needless to say, I was already well-known and well-respected with business partners and external stakeholders.

But, you know how it goes.

Translation?

They wanted to make sure no stone was left unturned in their quest to find someone—anyone—other than the Black woman who had:

- Already been doing the job unofficially for years ◇
- Designed the job they were hiring for

The interview process was… illuminating.

The interview: Three candidates, including myself.

1. A white male new to the organization with no risk, no regulatory compliance or assessment experience (10 years of project management experience)
2. A white female internal candidate (minimal risk experience)

3. And me (15 years of specialized experience in risk management, risk assessment, regulatory compliance, and controls, proven track record)

The interview panel: An all-white panel, inexperienced about risk, and junior to the role. Going into the interview, I was thinking, what kind of questions could they possibly ask me? They don't know what they don't know. The interview was over, and the feedback leaks started rolling in: "You are the most qualified, but you didn't interview well."

I had literally consulted on the enterprise-wide risk framework and designed the role, and outlined the requirements and skills for the role.

Something shifted in me as I was listening to this feedback. The executive who was less qualified than me—a white woman who at one time was my peer and who'd been in her role half as long as I'd been in mine and who I had encouraged to apply for her existing role and filled in gaps where she lacked experience—started questioning my abilities.

I felt that familiar pressure...

Smile.
Make them comfortable.
Don't appear 'aggressive' or come across 'angry.'
Play small.

Then I heard my grandmother's voice: *"Baby, excellence doesn't ask for permission."*

!The Shift.

I opened my portfolio, looked her dead in the eye, gave her a Tyra Banks 'smize,' and laid out the receipts:

Three major risk frameworks implemented $20.5M won in litigations through risk expertise. 99% issue management & resolution rate on my team. Enterprise Top Performer Award

I went into what I call my nice-ty response. You know, somewhere between nice and nasty where they don't know what hit them. My response—in a very calm and soft-spoken voice: "If you feel that feedback from inexperienced individuals outweighs the knowledge, expertise, and relationships that I bring to the table, and that I am truly not the right fit for the job, then you should base your decision solely on their feedback and not the known performance.

However, do not expect me to fill in the gap or train individuals who lack knowledge and expertise to lead the team and perform the role successfully," I said, my voice clear and confident. Line drawn.

The room got quiet. Real quiet.

She crinkled her forehead and raised an eyebrow.

But the real transformation came when I calmly leaned forward and said:

"You will be hard-pressed to find anyone—internal or external—who can do this job better than me."

I had already:

- Implemented similar strategies three years ago
- Delivered documented success metrics
- Built the internal & external relationships necessary for rapid implementation

The victory wasn't just getting the position.

It was about how I got it:

- Did not ask for permission
- Standing firmly in my expertise
- Refusing to minimize my achievements
- Leading with data and results
- Maintaining grace under pressure
- Willingness to bet on me and take the risk to stand up for me

The Impact as Risk Assessment & Controls Director:

- Implemented a new risk framework which was implemented globally
- Increased accuracy of risk identification and team diversity by 40%
- Established framework for risk assessment and identification of controls necessary to lift one of the largest government-implemented consent orders in history

But the real win? The day a young woman on my team told me, "Watching you in this role makes me believe it's possible for me too."

Journal Reflection:

When did you last dim your light to make others comfortable? What would you do differently now?

Remember:

- Your expertise is not up for debate
- Your experience has prepared you for this
- Your leadership is NEEDED
- Your success creates paths for others

The Seed Planted:

Every time you stand in your power, you water the gardens of possibility for those coming behind you.

As my grandmother would say: *"Baby, they can question your path, but they can't question your excellence."*

It's time. No more asking. No more waiting.

"You don't need permission to lead—so stop acting like you do."

Because that director's chair? It's not just a seat. It's a throne. And you were born to reign.

#WatchMeWork

That director's role wasn't just about professional advancement—it was about honoring every Black woman who had ever been told to wait her turn, to stay in her lane, to dream smaller.

III. The Roots: Ancestral Wisdom in Modern Times

"Excellence doesn't ask for permission—it shows up and shows out." – Grandpa's wisdom

Let me take you back to 2006, standing in my grandparents' kitchen in Dixie, Georgia. I had been fast-tracked for executive leadership after leading that game-changing information security project.

But let's be real—success wasn't without challenges.

I was now leading a team of highly-paid VPs, SVPs, and consultants—all white men who made more than me, their leader. Lord, the irony.

And none of them wanted to report to me.

One key leader refused to attend my meetings altogether.

I knew I had to navigate this situation fast, but the weight of being the only Black woman in the room sat heavy on my shoulders.

That's when I drove 458 miles over 7 hours to my grandparents' house for wisdom.

Kitchen Wisdom That Built Empires

My grandmother, who I affectionately called 'Mamma,' was making her famous sweet potato pie, moving with the rhythm of generations before her.

She didn't look up when she said, "Tell me what's troubling you, baby."

I let it spill out—the disrespect, the undermining, the constant pressure to prove myself.

She wiped her hands on her apron and pointed to the black and white photos on the wall—one of my grandfather, who I affectionately called 'Daddy,' and his cousin in their World War II uniforms and another of my great-grandmother.

"Let me tell you about where we came from," she said, pointing out the window to a 100-year-old building that had once been their schoolhouse and was now their church.

"Your grandfather and I went to that one-room schoolhouse. He only finished the 7th grade because he had to work and later go to war. I made it to the 10th grade. But that didn't stop him—he went on to own one of the first Black construction companies in South Florida, competing with white firms and winning contracts with businesses like Circle K."

She looked me dead in the eye:

"You think he wasn't scared?"

Then Daddy looked up from shelling peas on the sofa in the small living room and said:

"Baby, I decided I can show them better than I can tell them. I focused on being excellent and nurturing the right relationships in the right way. Sometimes, you have to set your ego aside and eat a little crow to impact change. Focus on knowing your job and theirs, and take nothing for granted. You are there because you deserve to be there—now show them why."

That was it. That was the lesson.

I had been waiting for them to acknowledge my authority, but now I understood: I didn't need their validation. I needed to walk in my greatness like it was already mine.

Family Lessons That Guide Me:

"Know Your History & Where You Come From"
Their photos weren't just decoration—they were receipts of resilience, excellence, and determination. That's why I always document everything and track my wins. When executives doubted me, I had the data, the receipts, and the metrics to prove my impact. Y'all don't understand...this strategy got me paid because I could quantify my impact on a trillion-dollar company.

"Make Your Presence Your Power"
Mamma had been a domestic worker in white homes. "But I carried myself like I owned every house I cleaned," she said. That stuck with me. Dignity isn't about your job title—it's about your presence.

"Build Your Table While You're Setting Theirs"
Grandpa soaked up every skill he could while working for others—and then he built his own empire. That's exactly what I did, using

my experience developing and implementing a strategy to launch my coaching and consulting business.

"Season Everything with Wisdom"
Mamma's cooking lesson wasn't just about pie. "Some people need more sugar, others need more spice. But never lose your flavor." In corporate America, I adjust my communication style without compromising who I am.

Reflection: What family wisdom guides your professional journey?
How are you honoring your ancestors in your work?
What legacy are you building for the next generation?

Our ancestors' wisdom lights the way, but in today's world, we need more than just their prayers—we need strategic sisterhood. Feel free to borrow my family's wisdom to guide you.

IV. The Circle: Building Your Power Base

"In corporate America and in business, a sister standing alone is a sister standing vulnerable."

Let me tell you about the day I learned that success isn't a solo sport.

It was the early 2000s, right before I took on the role as special project lead to fix the information security framework. I had been recruited from Internal Audit to the Technology Risk Group by a charismatic Black male leader.

But once I arrived, I quickly realized the team was in trouble. They weren't identifying critical risk issues, and worse—they didn't know how to fix them.

I had two choices:

- Raise my hand and fix it

- Stay silent and hope for the best

I raised my hand.

But here's the challenge: My leader's leader—the charismatic Black executive—lacked confidence to go against the grain. He was focused on what he perceived as them picking on him because he was a Black executive instead of getting the job done. As a result of raising my hand, I had been working 70-hour weeks consulting on risk strategy on top of my daily job to help him fix the problems.

And when he didn't implement the changes I recommended, external teams were brought in to assess the group.

I knew what was coming.

So, when the opportunity arose to join the Special Projects Team, I had to decide:

- Accept the role, knowing I'd face backlash from my previous executive
- Decline and likely be displaced

That's when I activated my Strategic Survival Squad.

The Power of Strategic Circles:

The Inner Circle – High-level allies & mentors provide guidance and protection from any backlashes that could derail your career.

The Strategy Circle – Subject-matter experts & legal advisors. Help with crafting your story and navigating legal obstacles if necessary to protect your reputation.

The Support Circle – Fellow Black women in leadership, prayer warriors, family council. Anytime you are taking risks, it can feel lonely and stressful.

Within 48 hours, my circles had:

- Secured my reporting structure
- Developed a communication strategy
- Created a framework for success

When I walked into that first meeting as Special Projects Lead, I wasn't alone. My circles had positioned me for success.

V. The Declaration: Your Time is NOW

Hear me clearly:

- A queen needs her court.
- A leader needs her allies.
- A champion needs her team.

Because the world doesn't need another silent queen. The world needs YOU—LOUD, PROUD, and CROWNED.

Now, go show them what your excellence looks like.

#WatchMeWork

Tivona Elliott

MEMOIR OF A MISFIT

R.O.A.R.ing To Greatness

3

MEMOIR OF A MISFIT

R.O.A.R.ING TO GREATNESS
By: Tivona Elliott

Principle: *Empower readers to embrace their uniqueness and rise to their greatness*

Stand on the threshold of the arena of your life, where the hum of anticipation is as palpable as the ground beneath your feet. This is your memoir, not penned in ink, but with the vivid hues of resolve, courage, and an indomitable will to R.O.A.R.—to rise above the scripted narratives and to claim the greatness that pulses through your veins. You are not a bystander in the chronicles of your existence; you are the protagonist, the misfit who does not conform but transforms.

This chapter is your manifesto, a call to arms for the soul that has been subdued by the murmurs of the past. We sear the principle of self-empowerment into these pages, offering a compass to navigate the labyrinth of your history and the roadmap to your glory. Each word is a heartbeat, each sentence a breath, drawing you closer to that sublime moment when you, too, will bask in the warmth of your own light.

As you walk through these sections, you will **Release Old Narratives** that have held you captive, shackling your potential in the cold, unforgiving chains of yesteryear. We dare you to look deeply into the well of your experiences, to draw from the waters of introspection, and to pour forth the elixir of a new story—a story that resonates with the timbre of your truth.

The journey will take you through valleys and over mountaintops as you **Overcome The Obstacles** that appear colossal only from a distance. Like an athlete whose muscles scream in protest, you will push through the pain, with each stride affirming your right to victory. You are not meant to tread lightly; you are meant to leave imprints so deep that they cannot be washed away by the tides of time.

In the silence of solitude, you will **Awaken The Rebel** that rages against the tyranny of the mundane. It is the rebel that challenges the status quo, the same fire that blazed in the hearts of those who dared to dream of something more beautiful than what the eyes have seen. The rebel is the spark, the catalyst for metamorphosis, urging you to unfurl the wings you were told you never had.

Finally, it is in the stillness of that awakening that you will **Rise To Greatness**, ascending not on the wings of angels but on the might of your own resolve. Greatness is not whispered; it is declared—a truth that reverberates through the canyons of your deepest fears and echoes back to you as an anthem of affirmation.

The promise we extend to you, the seeker, the warrior, the misfit, is a tapestry woven with threads of potential and possibility. Within these pages lie the echoes of a future where you are the architect, the sculptor, the composer of a life symphony that only you can conduct.

Let the words you read transform into actions, and the actions into a legacy.

The clock hands move, the pages turn, and you—yes, you—are ready. With a heart thundering against the odds, and a spirit that rises above the echoes of doubt, step into the realm where only the brave venture. Embrace the exquisite metamorphosis awaiting you, for this is your time to R.O.A.R. to greatness, and there is no symphony sweeter than that of a destiny fulfilled.

As you approach the dawn of this transformation, brace yourself for the catharsis of Release in the next section, where the shackles of old narratives begin to fall, and the canvas of your life awaits your triumphant stroke.

Release Old Narratives

As we forge onward from the precipice where hesitation and history entwine, we enter the realm where the echoes of the past reverberate. Here, the soil is fertile with the remnants of old stories, the ones scripted for us by the hands of others and our former selves. These tales have become heavy garments, ill-fitting and woven with the threads of outdated beliefs and fears that no longer serve us. It is time to shed them, to stand in the vulnerability of our naked truth, ready to write the memoirs of the misfit destined for greatness.

Imagine standing before an expansive mirror, the reflection returning your gaze not with the reality in which you live but with the illusions you've outgrown. In the courageous act of peering into this looking glass, you begin to unravel the narratives that have kept your greatness in the shadows. You've been a warrior in battles that weren't yours to fight and a dancer to music that never matched your heart's rhythm. Now, it's time to own your story, to release the old narratives and start anew.

You've carried the weight of judgment, of expectations, and the encompassing fear of judgment's piercing gaze. In its clutches, the voice that should have been your guiding force was muffled into submission. The world is rife with these crippling stories—they clip your wings, they mark out roads you never wished to travel, and they silence the symphony of your inner wisdom. We've all been there, a page in someone else's book, but now we tear out that page, crumple it, and allow the wind of change to carry it away. Your narrative is yours alone to pen.

With each step forward, feel the heavy chains of old narratives break and fall, clearing the path for your feet to carve new routes. These routes will have the imprint of your trials, the essence of your joy, and the testament of your commitment to rise. Here, we establish the cornerstone of who we wish to become, acknowledging the misfit within us that yearns not for normalcy, but for a life lived unapologetically and in vivid color. Our stories, once shackles, become our solace.

In shedding these layers, acknowledge the lessons they've taught. Gratitude for the past need not mean residence within it. Every tear, every setback, and every moment of doubt once shaped you but now gives you the foundation from which to soar. It's the paradox of growth: we rise higher when we acknowledge the ground from which we sprouted.

Reach deep, my fellow seeker, and with each word you read, let the ink dissolve what was, so that what will be can take its rightful shape. Today, you stand at the crossroads where resilience is born, and you will choose the path that leads towards a horizon ablaze with your very own brand of greatness.

As we cast away the tattered cloaks of our histories, brace yourself for the emergence of strength that defies barriers. We are not prisoners of our pasts, but architects of our future. Let the act of release be your clarion call to the world that you are coming, with the stories of old left as breadcrumbs for those who wish to follow your ascent. Carry forth this spirit, and let them marvel at the sight of obstacles not as hindrances, but as landmarks of your indomitable journey to greatness.

Overcome The Obstacles

The path to untold greatness is seldom a straight line; it is a trail blazed through the dense forest of challenges that stand robust, gnarled, and unyielding. Obstacles, both towering and subtle, have made their presence known in your journey. They are the seemingly insurmountable mountains and the deep, shadowy valleys that whisper your fears back to you in the stillness. They test your might, clasp your resolve, and beckon you to prove the strength of your inner compass. But behold, it is within this very proving ground that your spirit girds itself for the ascent you were born to make.

With the former narratives released like birds into the wide sky of possibility, you come, face-to-face, with the walls that barricade your path. These barriers—self-doubt, societal norms, the fangs of failure—seek to anchor you in place. Yet, they falter before your fierce resilience, for you know now the power that courses through your being. Each obstacle is a question, probing: "How fiercely do you yearn for your dreams?" And to this, you answer not with words, but with the valor of action, scaling the walls with an unwavering grip on your convictions.

The tales of yore that told of maidens waiting to be rescued were myths spun for the weary. You are the heroine of your saga, the savior of your own soul. And in this momentous epoch of your life, hurdles serve not to hinder, but to elevate—to teach you that the muscles of your aspirations grow sturdy under the weight of resistance. Remember, the fire that melts wax is the very same that tempers steel.

Each step over the rubble of conquered challenges is a testament to the indomitable will you wield. The dance of adversity is intricate, but you have learned its steps well. You stand unbroken in the torrent of life's trials, your victory cry resonating across the echoes of doubt that once populated the caverns of your mind. With every breath of resolve, you become your own alchemist, turning barriers into bridges, leading toward the golden sun of your most audacious goals.

You, who are both warrior and maven, have embarked on this hallowed trek, carrying the torch of transformation that ignites the potential lying dormant within. You are building a legacy with the mortar of perseverance and the blueprint of foresight. Your scars are your stars, charting out a constellation that narrates a saga of triumph, one that shows the way for those who dare to follow in your intrepid footsteps.

So push forward, relentless in your pursuit, consistent in your effort, even when the shadow of fatigue whispers the temptation of surrender. It is not in spite, but because of these challenges that your journey has depth, that your story gathers a richness that cannot be eroded with time. You are not just overcoming obstacles; you are crafting a masterpiece from the stone of resilience and the chisel of tenacity.

Let the fruition of your Released Old Narratives be the wind at your back as you face each obstacle. With the rise and fall of each conquered peak and trodden valley, forge ahead with a valor that startles the stillness, shaking loose the shackles of mediocrity. For your spirit, in its core, knows no bounds, finding vitality in the essence of challenge, and solace in the beauty of the climb.

And as you crest the top of the now-familiar hills of struggle, preparing to face the sun's glare on the other side, your eyes will search for the rebel you are about to Awaken. It slumbers, stirred by the drumbeat of your strides, ready to be roused—in you, the revolution of self-empowerment is nigh.

Awaken The Rebel

Amidst the tumultuous seas of change and the relentless skirmish against the bulwarks of old, there stirs an uprising—softly at first, like the murmur of the dormant earth before the quake. It is here, in the crucible of Overcoming Obstacles, that a simmering defiance blooms into a full-blown rebellion. The misfit, once clad in doubt's gray raiment, now dons the radiant armor of self-belief. The Rebel within awakens—a fierce maverick, an untamed spirit, the incarnation of unyielding determination.

This Rebel does not shriek in the alleys of discord nor hurl stones at the barricades of ignorance. No, this Rebel wields a mightier weapon—conscious choice, a resolute voice that declares, "No more!" to the status quo. With every breath, you unsheathe the sharp edge of discernment; you carve out a space in this world that cannot be filled by another, for it is uniquely and irrevocably yours.

Awakening the Rebel is a dance of flame and shadow. It is about finding the rhythm in chaos, the certainty in the ephemeral, the unwavering light in the darkest of nights. The Rebel thrives on the challenge, salivates at the prospect of overturning the tables of fate, and crafts a destiny forged in the crucible of personal vision.

The journey requires vigor, extracting from the depths a vitality that propels you past convention and hurtles you through the void of the commonplace. The air here is laced with the perfume of audacious dreams, stirred to life by the flapping wings of your unshackled aspirations. Embrace this insurgence with open arms and a fierce heart, for it is in this act of rebellion that your true purpose is honed to a razor's edge.

This Rebel is not a prisoner of circumstance. Cast aside the chains of 'what has been'; forge instead the links of 'what will be', an unbreakable chain of actions and consequences, dreams and realities interlocked in an unending cycle of growth. You glean wisdom from the debris of battles fought and won, fueling your insurrection with a resolute clarity that no shroud of doubt can dim.

Through the Awakening, you gain a comrade in arms—the purest version of yourself, one not swayed by the allure of banal triumphs but inspired by the symphony of transcendent victories that resonate with the core of your essence. This alliance is your beacon, illuminating the path to a fulfillment that cannot be contained within the parameters of ordinary existence.

The outer world, once a cacophony of competing dogmas, now dances to the tune of your indomitable will. The Rebel, with astute awareness, discerns the call to action amidst the noise. There is a promise in the wind, a narrative of purpose written on the scroll of the horizon, beckoning you to inscribe the rest of your story in bold, unapologetic strokes.

As this Rebel crescendos within, pounding at the walls of limitation, a monumental shift transpires within the chambers of your deepest self. Behold, the reflection in the mirror transforms, no longer a mirage weighed down by the gravity of the past, but a portrait of empowerment personified, electric with potential and magnetic with resolve.

This awakening is your dawn chorus, a rebel's ballad sung at the intersection of yesterday's lessons and tomorrow's freedoms. And as the final notes linger in the swelling light, you find that your newfound rebellion has charted a course, set sail toward a destiny where you stand as the captain at the helm, and the Rise To Greatness that awaits is but the next step in your odyssey towards a legacy written in the stars—undaunted, unyielding, unparalleled.

Rise To Greatness

The dawn of a new era is upon us, where the awakened Rebel archetype strides across the threshold of becoming, a sculptor of the future. Here, in this sacred space of transformation where passion and purpose collide, you, the undying Misfit, Rise To Greatness. It's not a quiet ascension, nor one marked by the tepid claps of faint admirers. No, this Rise is a resounding crescendo, a clarion call that resounds through the halls of creation, heralding the arrival of a titan.

Behold the luminosity of your essence, now unfurling like a banner across the skyline of achievements untold. Your journey has been a crucible in which the raw ore of your mettle has been refined, transformed into a lustrous beacon of excellence. In this act of Rising, you transcend barriers, shattering the glass ceilings with a resonance that sends shards of the once-impenetrable tumbling down like relics of a conquered era.

With each stride up the mountainside of legacy, your feet tread upon the sediment of trials long endured. The once jagged rocks that cut your heels now serve as stepping stones, polished smooth by perseverance and resilience. At this summit, the view is not one that inspires mere awe—it is a reflection of the world that awaits your fierce grace to reshape it.

Rise, for the world has far too long been parched, yearning for the quenching rains of your wisdom, the flowing rivers of your insights. Rise, for the bellows of the furnace that forged your spirit are now the trumpets of your victory, the symphony of your sovereignty. Rise, for every soul that has glimpsed your light finds within themselves an ember, igniting their own paths to greatness.

Greatness, in this sacred lexicon of warriors and poets, is more than a destination—it is an eternal pursuit. It is an unbroken vow to honor the vibrance within, an unyielding commitment to manifest the visions that once danced in the silhouettes of dreams. Let the horizons of the past be the backdrops against which you paint the constellations of tomorrow's triumphs.

In this Rise, you are the architect, the engineer and the bricklayer of your fortunes. Each goal achieved, every ceiling shattered, serves as a testament to the boundless arenas of your capabilities. The communities you build, the lives you inspire, and the echoing impact of your actions stand as monuments to the power you wield.

The significance of this Rise cannot be captured in the transient ink of headlines or the fleeting flashes of camera lights. It is etched into the annals of time, each word a stepping stone for those who will walk the path you've blazed. The future generations will speak your name with reverence, each syllable a beacon that guides them through the tempestuous journey of their own becoming.

Yet, as you stand at this zenith, the twilight whispers of dawn beckon. The tapestry of your legacy, vibrant and ever-expanding, stretches forward into realms uncharted. The journey continues, and with it, the ascent escalates, for the Rise To Greatness knows no finale, no curtain call. It beckons you onward, toward horizons only dreamt of, toward peaks that pierce the celestials.

From this vantage point, the odyssey stretches out before you—a panoramic vista of what lies ahead. Your heart, an indomitable drum, beats to the rhythm of forward motion, your eyes alight with the fire of purpose and passion. The air hums with anticipation; the cosmos itself holds its breath, for it knows the magnitude of the voyage you embark upon. It is more than a journey—it is a magnificent flight toward the FleX, an expanse where the only constant is transcendence, and the only truth is the boundless sky of potential that sprawls endlessly beyond.

Cultivating Courageous Compassion

Beneath the expansive sky of potential, as you Rise To Greatness, let us not forget the fertile ground from which such a towering tree has emerged. The roots of courage have delved deep, drawing sustenance from the wellspring of your every trial and triumph. The might of your reach, the breadth of your canopy, is a sanctuary not just for your own dreams, but a refuge for others navigating their storms. In Cultivating Courageous Compassion, you become the embodiment of strength serving a purpose greater than self—a beacon of hope and a testament to the power inherent in the alchemy of empathy and action.

Encounter each soul with the same indomitable spirit that propelled your own ascent. See in them the mirror of your past, the kindred essence of aspiration, the shared thirst for a life unbound by limitations. Shepherd them with words that carry the weight of genuine concern interlaced with the wisdom of your journey. Forge connections that vibrate with the authenticity of lived experiences, forging a collective that rises in tandem, a tapestry of transformation spun from a multitude of threads.

Therein lies the truest barometer of greatness: not in the solitary summits scaled but in the hearts uplifted, the lives irrevocably changed by the gravity-defying leap of faith inherent in your story. For what is a legacy but the ripples of kindness reverberating through epochs long after our voices have melded with the winds of time?

Within your compassionate embrace, mentorship becomes a forge where the once fragile iron of uncertainty transmutes into steel, resilience wrought in the crucible of your guiding light. Your narrative now serves as a map for those traversing the labyrinth of their self-doubt, the ink of your trials a navigation aid through their densest fogs.

With each act of courageous compassion, you craft a lineage—not of blood, but of spirit—a dynasty where every individual is sovereign over their destiny, where tales of triumph are currency, and perseverance the crown jewel. The constellations you chart in this vast cosmos of interconnectivity become the stars by which future generations will navigate, their inheritance a universe where possibility is the only horizon.

As your saga continues, the song of your deeds marries the rhythm of change with the melody of solidarity, creating an anthem for the ages. Your journey becomes less about the heights you have conquered and more about the multitude you have uplifted, the paradigm you've shifted, transforming what it means to be great.

This greatness, raw and resplendent, is not characterized by rigidity but by fluidity—the fluidity of benevolence, of strength that softens in the presence of sorrow, of power that bends but never breaks in the face of another's pain. It is a manifestation of character, honor, and the empathetic resonance that hallmarks all true leaders.

In this chapter of your narrative, as you continue to soar, remember the wind beneath your wings—the shared hopes and collective aspirations of your brethren, their victories your own. The horizon—once a boundary—now challenges you with new purpose, inviting you to rediscover yourself in the reflection of the lives you've touched, in the stories you've become a part of.

And so, with every heartbeat that drums in harmony with the Rise To Greatness, let the echo carry forth a new creed. A declaration that greatness is not a mantle worn in solitary pride, but a quilt woven from the multihued fabric of humanity, wrapped around the shoulders of the world—warm, generous, and everlasting.

As the canvas of your journey unfurls onto the world stage, we crest the edge, peering into the vast unknown. With the same pioneering spirit that has marked every step of your path, let us transcend the familiar, venturing now with audacious grace toward the spaces that beckon us to redefine, to reimagine, to FleX. Here, within this next chapter, we find ourselves at the nexus of change—a threshold promising a renaissance of thought and a revolution in being.

Embracing The Tapestry of Triumph

As we stand within the fertile soil of our cultivated courageous compassion, we recognize that the tapestry we weave with the vibrant threads of our lives is more than a mere fabric—it is an emblem of triumph. Every stitch is a tale of resilience, each pattern a chapter of victory in the grand narrative that is our existence. As Misfits who have dared to challenge the status quo, who've defied the gravity of expectations, we've learned to embrace life's vast spectrum, painting our journey with bold and unapologetic strokes of brilliance and grace.

The mosaic of courage that we've crafted is replete with the hues of every storm weathered, every battle won. The richness lies not in a monochrome of uniformity, but in the polychromatic beauty of diversity—of experiences embraced, stories told, and lessons learned. Each piece, when melded with another, reinforces the whole, creating a masterpiece robust enough to withstand the perturbations of any tempest or the shadows of any eclipse.

Our past—rich with the wisdom of yesteryears—is the crucible where our mettle was tested, forming an unbreakable chain of connection to the present. This present moment, the fulcrum of our existence, balances the weight of history with the prospect of a future radiant with promise. And as we chart our course forward, it is with the knowledge that each experience, each misstep or stride forward, is a vital chord in the symphony of our Rise To Greatness.

We are the maestros of our fate, harnessing the harp of destiny, our fingers deftly coaxing forth melodies both haunting and exuberant. The music of our lives resonates within the chambers of collective memory, inspiring listeners who, with bated breath, await the next note of our ever-evolving opus. Challenges that once seemed insurmountable now become verses of valiance, refrains that resonate with the power of our newfound strength and clarity.

The cadence of our days, once erratic, now pulses with intention and mindful synchronicity. We cast aside the chains of old, whose links were forged in the fires of doubt and fear. Now, in their stead, we adorn ourselves with the medallions of self-discovery, each a testament to the journey within and the battle won.

Rise, for in this act, you proclaim that each day is an opportunity to sculpt the self anew, to etch upon the sands of time a legacy that will endure. With the winds of change at your back and the sunlight of enlightenment guiding your path, embrace the tapestry of your triumph with the reverence it deserves. It is your proclamation, your declaration of independence from all that once sought to contain your boundless spirit.

We look to the horizon, not as a distant dream, but as a new day brimming with opportunity—a day where the amalgam of our passions, our skills, our dreams, becomes the crucible from which innovation and authenticity pour forth. We are no longer confined by the imagery of what was; we become the artists of what will be, painting with the colors of audacity, wisdom, and an unstoppable resolve.

In this dance of life, where every step is both choreographed and spontaneous, we find beauty in the fluidity, majesty in the movement. It is in the embrace of both shadow and light that we discover the full spectrum of our humanity and the undeniable strength it embodies.

And now, as we transition from one canvas to the next, let us carry with us the richness of our past achievements, the knowledge that we are forever students and teachers in this grand academy of life. Armed with the courage to flex against the conventional, to bend the narrative arcs toward a future crafted by our own hands, we ready ourselves to embark on a new chapter—our daring odyssey continues where boundaries are redefined and the narratives are stitched with the golden threads of newfound resilience.

F.R.E.E.—Finding Resilience in Every Experience. This is not just a mantra; it is a quest, a discovery, a formula that propels us from the adversity that has tempered our spirit to the triumphs that await. Here, within this unfolding treasure trove of wisdom and wonder, we begin to flourish. For in this new chapter, we are the cartographers mapping out our journey from overcoming to owning, from the shadows of yesterday to the brilliant dawn of tomorrow.

Tinesha Boswell

F.R.E.E.
Finding Resilience in Every Experience

4

F.R.E.E.

FINDING RESILIENCE IN EVERY EXPERIENCE
By: Tinesha Boswell

Dr. Tinesha Boswell is a certified wellness coach, mental health specialist, and founder of i.P.U.S.H Wellness Coaching and Consulting, where she helps women transform their lives through mindset, nutrition, and fitness.

Drawing from her own journey of overcoming health challenges while building a successful coaching practice, she teaches women to Persevere, embrace their Uniqueness, find Solidarity, and maintain Hope.

Her chapter in Girl, There's a Champion in You demonstrates how focusing on wellness and refusing to give up can lead to profound personal transformation.

As the author of "Don't Give Up Too Soon" and Lead Ambassador for TrulyWedWives Society, Dr. Boswell continues to inspire women to fight for their best lives in mind, body, and soul. Connect with her at ipushwellness.com.

"In the midst of darkness, the light within us shines the brightest" - Unknown author

Principle: Resilient Transformation: Resilience is not just about enduring hardships but about finding strength, healing, and purpose through compassion and grace. This journey involves illuminating our inner light, seeking holistic healing, embracing new beginnings, and maintaining resilience through reflection and intentional action.

By embodying these principles, we transform adversity into opportunities for growth, becoming beacons of hope and light for ourselves and others.

LIFE:

Girlfriend, let me tell you something. Life ain't always a smooth ride, but it's in those bumpy moments that we find our true strength. I'm Tinesha, and I'm here to share with you how we can be F.R.E.E - Finding Resilience in Every Experience.

This isn't just about surviving, it's about thriving; even when the world feels like it's crumbling around us.

As Black women, we carry the weight of generations on our shoulders. We're the rocks of our families, the pillars of our communities.

But who holds us up when we're close to falling? That's what we're going to explore together.

We're going to learn how to shine our light even in the darkest of times, how to heal ourselves body and soul, and how to keep that flame of resilience burning bright.

As you read this, take a moment to reflect on what you've learned throughout this chapter. Consider the following questions and write your thoughts in a journal:

1. What aspect of the chapter resonated with you the most, and why?
2. How do you plan to implement the strategies and tools discussed in your own life?
3. What have you discovered about your own resilience through these reflections?
4. In what ways can you continue to build resilience in every experience you encounter?

So buckle up, sis. We're about to embark on a journey of transformation, one that will take us from bearing burdens to breaking free. Are you ready? Let's dive in.

The Weight of the World: Bearing the Burden with Grace

As I sit here thinking about my parents, I realize that life doesn't always provide us with the choices we feel it right. When my mom got sick, I realized that I had to find a way to live without and that was a thought that I could not commit to but had no choice.

I was really worried about my dad. Following my mom's death, my dad was in a car accident that should have killed him, but it didn't. We had to ask the hospital to release my dad so he could make it to her viewing.

A few months later, I lost my job, and my dad was diagnosed with his first cancer. That was when I realized that my journey was no longer mine. I stopped doing business so I could make sure I was present for my dad. That's when my journey to healing and taking care of others began.

The journey of caring for loved ones who were battling sickness and eventually passed away was one of the most challenging periods of my life. Among them were my parents, a few friends, and my mother-in-law.

Despite the overwhelming burden, I chose to bear it with grace and compassion, determined to be a beacon of light for them in their darkest hours.

Losing multiple loved ones in such a short span of time was devastating. There were moments when the weight of the world felt unbearable, and I questioned how much more I could endure. But in those moments of doubt, I found strength in God, which allowed me to be a source of joy and comfort for my family.

When dad and my two friends were struggling, music was what brought them joy. I would dance, sing, or just listen to their favorite songs. Watching them smile in the midst of their dying gave me much joy and happiness. It showed me that you can live even when you are dying.

"The greatest glory in living lies not in never falling, but in rising every time we fall" - Nelson Mandela

The Beacon of Resilience: Shining through Adversity

When dealing with loved ones who are gravely ill, it can be incredibly challenging to stay positive because the sickness is all-consuming, obscuring the person they once were. However, I found strength by recalling the vibrant and resilient individuals they were before their illness.

My mom, for instance, was the epitome of resilience and care. A homemaker in every sense, she cooked, cleaned, and ensured we were always taken care of regardless of how she was feeling. Growing up as an asthmatic, I spent significant time in hospitals, often away from home. My mom was there every step of the way, regardless of her own exhaustion or health struggles.

Even when my mom's health declined, weighing just 60 pounds, I focused on bringing joy into her life. We watched her favorite TV shows together, laughed, and reminisced about the good times. Similarly, with friends who were ill, I engaged in activities that brought them happiness. One friend loved to dance, so we danced. Another enjoyed talking, so we had long conversations.

"Even in the darkest moments, we can find light by remembering the love and strength that have always surrounded us."

Healing and Strength: Embracing Therapy and Physical Wellness

My journey with holistic healing was enhanced before my mother's death. She struggled with severe stomach issues, which were initially diagnosed as IBS. Despite numerous treatments and medications, she endured constant pain and digestive problems. Her health deteriorated rapidly because of poor health issues, leading to an emotional and physical decline.

When my mom passed away, my husband urged me to take care of myself and seek therapy. I resisted at first, thinking I could handle it on my own. But he was right; I needed help. As a mental health coach, it took a lot to be a beginner again.

I had to set aside my knowledge and allow myself to be vulnerable. Therapy became a crucial part of my healing process.

The biggest impact that helped me was my therapist taking me through an exercise using my 5 senses. She told me that whenever I felt overwhelmed, crying, or exhausted, to take at least 5 minutes to just breathe (smelling essential oils is how I usually did it).

I would also listen to jazz music while looking out of the window at beautiful flowers. On the real challenging days, I would squeeze a stress ball and sip on some tea or water. Five years later, I am still using these techniques.

Exercise also played a significant role in my healing journey. I started the "Morning Meltdown 100" program with Beachbody On Demand. This 100-day workout program became a source of strength and stability for me. Each session was a way to honor my mom and fight for my health.

The routine I established—waking up early, exercising, reading, and journaling—helped me process my emotions and maintain a sense of normalcy. I still, to this day get up at 5 A. M. to exercise with my group.

"He heals the brokenhearted and binds up their wounds." - Psalm 147

A New Dawn: From Light to Liberation

When my dad first got sick, my husband realized that we will need to live closer to help him on his cancer journey. He was struggling badly with the death of my mom. All my dad knew was how to work and take care of his family. Once mom passed, he lost his purpose, and once he was unable to work, he felt like he lost his life and there was nothing else to live for.

Being closer to my dad showed him that he was not alone and he had family to lean on. Dad's Prostate Cancer was cured, but then tragically, he was diagnosed with stage 4 Pancreatic Cancer. He lived for 10 months following that diagnosis. My husband's mom passed away a few months later.

From that point, our lives changed drastically. Neither of us had our parents to talk to or to lean on. Philly was getting worse, and my husband was ready for a change.

In July 2022, we took a leap of faith and moved from Philadelphia to South Carolina. We lived with my sister for a few months until we found a home to rent. Eventually, we may purchase a home, but right now, we love where we are.

We are in love with our new journey. We can enjoy our moments of peace when we sit outside.

People wave when you walk or drive by them. The atmosphere is definitely different from what we were used to, but it's something we can get behind. Don't be afraid to take a leap of faith when you know it's time to pivot.

Here are tips for embracing change and building resilience.

1. **Acknowledge and Accept Change:** Recognize that change is an inevitable part of life. Accepting change rather than resisting it can reduce stress and open up new opportunities for growth.
2. **Develop a Support Network:** Surround yourself with supportive friends, family, and community members. Sharing your experiences and feelings can provide emotional relief and practical advice.
3. **Cultivate a Positive Mindset:** Focus on the positive aspects of change and how it can lead to new opportunities. Reframe challenges as chances to learn and grow.
4. **Practice Self-Care:** Taking care of your physical, emotional, and mental health is crucial during times of change. Incorporate activities that rejuvenate and relax you, such as exercise, reading, or meditation.

5. **Set Goals and Take Action:** Setting small, achievable goals can help you feel more in control and provide a sense of direction. Break down large goals into manageable steps.

Keeping the Flame Alive: Strategies for Enduring Through Milestones

Free Your Mind: Embracing Mental Resilience Reflect: Think about a time when your mind felt overwhelmed by challenges. Write down the thoughts that were holding you back and how you overcame them.

a. Homework: Create a list of positive affirmations that you can repeat daily to strengthen your mental resilience.

b. Scripture: "Do not conform to the pattern of this world, but be transformed by the renewing of your mind.

Then you will be able to test and approve what God's will is—his good, pleasing and perfect will." (Romans 12:2)

Free Your Spirit: Cultivating Spiritual Resilience Reflect: Consider a spiritual practice or belief that has helped you through tough times. How has it provided comfort and strength?

a. Homework: Dedicate a few minutes each day to a spiritual practice, whether it's meditation, prayer, or reading inspirational texts.

b. Scripture: "The Lord is my shepherd, I lack nothing. He makes me lie down in green pastures, he leads me beside quiet waters, he refreshes my soul." (Psalm 23:1-3)

Free Your Emotions: Harnessing Emotional Resilience Reflect: Identify an emotional challenge you faced and how you managed to cope with it. What emotions were the hardest to deal with, and how did you find balance?

a. Homework: Keep an emotional journal for a week, noting down your feelings and how you address them. Identify patterns and areas for growth.

b. Scripture: "He heals the brokenhearted and binds up their wounds." (Psalm 147:3)

Free Your Body: Building Physical Resilience Reflect: Recall a time when your physical health was tested. How did you overcome the physical challenges, and what did you learn about your body's strength and limits?

a. Homework: Develop a simple exercise routine or a health goal that you can commit to, aiming to enhance your physical resilience.

b. Scripture: "Do you not know that your bodies are temples of the Holy Spirit, who is in you, whom you have received from God?

You are not your own; you were bought at a price. Therefore, honor God with your bodies." (1 Corinthians 6:19-20)

Free Your Environment: Creating Social and Environmental Resilience

Reflect: Think about your social and physical environment. How do these spaces and relationships support or hinder your resilience?

a. Homework: Make a plan to declutter a space in your home and cultivate relationships that uplift and support you.

b. Scripture: "Therefore encourage one another and build each other up, just as in fact you are doing." (1 Thessalonians 5:11)

In our journey towards Finding Resilience in Every Experience (F.R.E.E), it's essential to celebrate our small victories and nourish ourselves from the inside out, thriving, even in the face of adversity.

Resilience Reviver Mocktail and Benefits:

The mocktail combines sparkling water for hydration and detoxification, lemon juice to boost the immune system and aid digestion, and ginger to reduce inflammation and improve digestive health.

Honey provides natural energy and soothes the throat, while mint leaves offer a refreshing taste and aid in digestion, promoting calmness and tranquility.

Enjoy this drink as a symbol of clarity, renewal, and strength on your journey towards resilience.

Ingredients:

- 1 cup green tea (calming and full of antioxidants)
- 1/2 cup coconut water (hydrating and replenishing)
- 1/4 cup pomegranate juice (rich in antioxidants)
- Juice of 1 lemon (boosts immunity and detoxifies)
- 1 tsp honey (natural sweetener and anti-inflammatory)
- Fresh mint leaves (refreshing and aid digestion)

Instructions:

1. Brew green tea and let it cool.
2. In a pitcher, combine green tea, coconut water, pomegranate juice, lemon juice, and honey. Stir well.
3. Pour over ice and garnish with fresh mint leaves.
4. Enjoy this refreshing mocktail that symbolizes resilience and renewal.

Benefits of Each Ingredient:

- Green Tea: Calms the mind and is rich in antioxidants, promoting overall health.

- Coconut Water: Hydrates and replenishes electrolytes, keeping you energized.
- Pomegranate Juice: Loaded with antioxidants, it protects your body from free radicals.
- Lemon Juice: Boosts immunity and aids in detoxification.
- Honey: Natural sweetener with anti-inflammatory properties.
- Mint Leaves: Refreshing and aids in digestion.

This mocktail represents the essence of being F.R.E.E. – finding resilience in every experience. Enjoy it as a symbol of your journey towards resilience and transformation.

Take a moment to reflect on what you've learned throughout this chapter. Consider the following questions and write your thoughts in a journal:

a. **What I Learned About Myself:** Reflect on your journey and the steps you've taken towards healing. How have these practices impacted your resilience? What new strengths have you discovered?
b. **Resonating Aspects:** Identify the parts of this journey that resonated most deeply with you. How can you incorporate these insights into your daily life?
c. **Growth Through Trials and Tribulations:** Consider the challenges you've faced. How have these experiences shaped your resilience? What steps will you take to continue growing and thriving despite adversity?

Scripture: Isaiah 40:31 (NIV): "But those who hope in the Lord will renew their strength. They will soar on wings like eagles; they will run and not grow weary, they will walk and not be faint." Reflect on this scripture and how it applies to your journey towards resilience and finding strength in every experience.

As we close this chapter on finding resilience, we open the door to new possibilities. In the next chapter, "The Fall: The Void: The Rise," we'll explore how these moments of resilience prepare us for the inevitable falls in life, guide us through the void of uncertainty, and ultimately lead us to rise stronger than ever before. Remember, girlfriend, your journey of transformation is ongoing. The resilience you've discovered here is just the beginning.

Tamara Rivers

THE FALL-THE VOID-THE RISE

The Quest for the Unveiled Self
Embracing the Past Shaping the Future

5

THE FALL-THE VOID-THE RISE

THE QUEST FOR THE UNVEILED SELF
EMBRACING THE PAST
SHAPING THE FUTURE

By: Tamara Rivers

The Symphony of Self-Discovery

Listen up, beautiful soul! This chapter is your anthem, your battle cry, your declaration of independence from the chains of your past. We're about to embark on a journey that'll shake you to your core and lift you higher than you've ever been.

This is for every young Black woman who's ever felt the weight of a bad decision, who's ever looked in the mirror and seen disappointment staring back.

But here's the truth bomb: this journey isn't just about overcoming; it's about unveiling. It's about peeling back the layers of doubt, fear, and regret to reveal the radiant, powerful woman you've always been underneath. This is your quest for the unveiled self.

Remember this: Your story isn't over. It's just beginning. You are not the sum of your mistakes. You are a force of nature, a symphony of strength, resilience, and untapped potential. By embracing your past-yes, even the parts that make you wince-you're shaping a future that's brighter than anything you've ever imagined.

As we dive into The Fall, The Void, and The Rise, keep this principle close to your heart: every step of your journey, even the missteps, is part of unveiling your true self. It's about turning your losses into lessons, your pain into power, and your story into a beacon of hope for others.

Let's turn up the volume on your life and let the world hear your roar! It's time to embrace your past, shape your future, and unveil the magnificent, unstoppable force that is you!

The Fall - Introduction to the Protagonist

Baby girl, it's time to face the music. The Fall isn't about hitting rock bottom; it's about facing your truth head-on. It's about looking your past in the eye and saying, "You don't control me anymore."

It was the year 1989, and I was only 16 years old. In love with this very attractive guy, five years older than I was. All the girls on the block wanted to talk to him, but he chose me. I had never dated or even kissed a boy, and yet he wanted me. I felt flattered, so I took his hand, and man, I was in for the ride of my life.

At just 16 years old, he brought me all kinds of designer clothes and bags, and those bags weren't empty—they were filled with cash, sometimes $500 to $1,000. He spoiled me, and I loved it. I was a daddy's girl; my father was very active in my life. In fact, I was the only kid on the block who lived with both parents.

Before dealing with him, I was an A/B student. But the attention I received felt so good. I remember my dad one day asking, "Where did you get that outfit from?" I couldn't tell him, but the next thing he said was, "Do not accept gifts from this boy, because once you do, he'll think he owns you. And if that happens... I want you to give everything back. NOW."

Well, he gave me two human beings that I couldn't give back. By the time I was 18 years old, I had two children by him. He had become very controlling and sometimes even abusive. My life, as I knew it, was over.

My dad was very disappointed, and my mother tried her best to shield me from the hurt I was feeling because I once had dreams—dreams of becoming a lawyer. My dreams and hopes had died. Now, I had two boys looking up at me, but I was still a child myself with a crazy baby daddy.

What is a young lady supposed to do?

Your early choices might have painted your world in shades of regret, but listen closely: those colors are just the underpainting of your masterpiece.

You felt like an embarrassment, searching for validation in all the wrong places. But here's the truth bomb: your worth isn't determined by anyone else's opinion of you.

As Ledisi would say, it's time for a "Piece of Mind." Your past doesn't define you; it refines you. It's the grit that's going to polish you into the diamond you were always meant to be.

The Void - Living in the Shadows

Now, let's talk about The Void. That dark place where losing became your normal, where you started anticipating failure before you even tried. Girl, I see you. I feel you. But it's time to step out of those shadows.

For years, self-doubt was my constant companion. After having my first two children at such a young age, I began to see myself as a failure. Let's get it clear - not my babies. They made me who I am. Every dream I once had seemed impossible, and I thought that my choices had permanently sealed my fate.

I would look at my boys, knowing I had to be strong for them, but deep down, I felt broken, overwhelmed, and unsure of how to pick up the pieces.

It wasn't until I hit rock bottom—being stalked by my kid's father for over a year, losing apartment after apartment because of him- and being financially tapped out—that I realized something had to change. I couldn't keep living in fear of what I couldn't do.

The day I chose not to drown anymore, I had no choice but to take responsibility, not just for my children, but for my future too. That's when I made a decision. I started small, setting simple goals, and celebrating every step forward, no matter how small.

I enrolled in college and slowly rebuilt my confidence. Each new achievement, no matter how minor, chipped away at the self-doubt that had kept me stagnant for so long. I began to see that I wasn't defined by my past mistakes. More importantly, I started to believe that I could create the future I wanted, not just for me but for my children too.

One of the most transformative moments came when I finished a college course that I thought I wouldn't be able to handle. It wasn't the class itself that changed me—it was the realization that I could still learn, still grow, and still rise. For the first time in years, I felt in control of my life again.

Now, whenever self-doubt creeps in, I remind myself of everything I've already overcome. I went from a scared young girl who thought her life was over to a woman who is determined to build a future for herself and her children. That journey continues every day, but I know now that I am more than capable.

The Void isn't your home; it's just a temporary stop on your journey. It's the cocoon where you're transforming, where you're shedding the skin of your old self. In the words of Mary J. Blige, "No more drama." It's time to rewrite your story.

Remember, playing it safe might keep you from falling, but it also keeps you from flying. Your comfort zone? It's a beautiful place, but nothing ever grows there.

The Rise - Turning Losses into Lessons

This is it, queen. The Rise. This is where you take those L's and turn them into lessons. This is where you look at every setback and say, "Watch me bounce back."

Looking back, I realize my journey as a leader started much earlier than I thought. At the age of 20, while working my first job at Hardee's, my manager saw something in me that I hadn't yet recognized. They promoted me to a managerial role and said, "You're a true leader."

From that moment on, in every job I held, I was always seen as the go-to person—the one who could get the job done.

After completing my bachelor's degree in business with a minor in Legal Studies, I secured a position as a foreclosure paralegal at a law firm. I worked there for over two years, gaining valuable skills and insight into the legal process.

Unfortunately, I was let go, but rather than seeing it as a setback, I viewed it as an opportunity to take the training and experience I had gained and apply it elsewhere.

I found my calling when I began working for a nonprofit organization that was awarded funding to help save homeowners from foreclosure. During my time at the law firm, I had been the one drafting complaints and ensuring clients were served.

Now, I could use that same knowledge to educate homeowners about their rights and help them save their homes. It felt like I had found my purpose—giving back to my community.

Managing a team of five, we traveled across the state of South Carolina, hosting foreclosure clinics and providing much-needed assistance to those facing financial hardship. Over time, we were able to save over 2,000 homes and return $16.1 million to the state.

Helping people keep their homes was more than just a job—it was a mission. Every family we helped was a reminder that my journey, from Hardee's to law firms to nonprofit work, had equipped me to make a real difference in people's lives. Now, I am CEO of The Financial Transformation, where I educate individuals and Business owners on how to master their finances one $ at a time.

You're not just surviving anymore; you're thriving. You're not just existing; you're living with purpose. Like Taraji P. Henson says, "The sky is not the limit. Your mind is."

Every loss you've experienced? It's just been preparation for your victories. Every tear you've cried? It's watering the seeds of your success. You're not just rising; you're soaring.

My vision for empowering others is deeply rooted in the lessons I've learned from my own journey. I've experienced both triumphs and setbacks, moments of self-doubt, and times of extraordinary growth.

Through it all, I've come to realize that true empowerment begins when we see our challenges not as obstacles, but as opportunities to learn, evolve, and rise stronger.

Having been given chances to lead, to learn, and to transform, I now see it as my mission to create spaces where others can do the same. Whether it's through financial education, personal development, or helping someone find their way after a setback, my goal is to provide the tools and support that will enable people to take control of their lives and futures.

I want to show others that failure is not the end—it's just a chapter in their story. Through programs, mentorship, and community-building efforts, my vision is to help individuals see their own potential, even when they can't see it themselves. I believe everyone has the power to break through barriers, rewrite their narrative, and pursue the life they truly deserve.

The growth I've experienced—from being a young mother facing uncertainty to leading teams that have saved thousands of homes, to being CEO of my company—fuels my desire to lift others up. My vision is to foster a society where no one feels trapped by their circumstances, and everyone has access to the resources, knowledge, and encouragement they need to thrive.

Empowerment, to me, is about more than just helping someone solve a problem—it's about instilling confidence, resilience, and a belief in their own worth. I envision a future where the lessons I've learned are shared, so that others can overcome their challenges and create new possibilities for themselves and their communities.

Your Unfolding Story

Beautiful, brave, brilliant sister – this is just the beginning of your story. You're writing a narrative of resilience, courage, and unshakable confidence with every choice you make, every challenge you overcome, and every goal you crush.

As you step into your power, know that you're not just changing your own life – you're changing the world. You're redefining what it means to be a young Black woman in this society. You're showing the next generation what's possible when you believe in yourself and refuse to be limited by anyone else's expectations.

So go forth and conquer, my rising star. Your time is now. Your moment is here. The world is waiting for the gift that only you can give. Shine on!

Monique Howell

UNCHAINED

The Sojourn Through Sickness to Social Triumph

6

UNCHAINED

A SOJOURN THROUGH SICKNESS TO SOCIAL TRIUMPH

By: Monique Howell

True healing and resilience begin within, transforming personal struggles into sources of strength and social change.

In the stillness before dawn, when the world holds its breath in anticipation of a new day, a profound truth echoes in the chambers of the heart. It is here, in this sacred space, that healing begins.

The resilience that carries us through darkness into light finds its first breath within, in the uncharted terrains of the soul.

As a Black woman navigating the complexities of life with HIV, I've learned that healing transcends the physical. It's a spiritual and emotional odyssey, a reclamation of narrative, worth, and place in the world. This chapter is for you, the resilient warrior at life's crossroads. It's a beacon, signaling safe passage through tumultuous seas.

A specific moment when I realized the importance of my inner healing was when I didn't know my own self-worth. I was crying and screaming in silence, wanting people to hear me, but I was too afraid to let go, ashamed because in my mind I thought I failed my family, even myself.

I realized I had to heal and that nobody can do that for me but me!

Remember, your worth is immeasurable. As Maya Angelou once said, "You may encounter many defeats, but you must not be defeated."

Let these words be your mantra as we embark on this journey together.

Mental Awareness:

The Gateway to Self-Empowerment

The pursuit of mental clarity is akin to scaling a mountain. With each step, each revelation of thought and release of fear, you ascend. You rise, not to escape the world below, but to gain perspective—a vantage point from which you can survey your life with wisdom and serenity.

As a nurse practitioner and a single mother, I intimately understand the weight of responsibilities that can cloud our minds. The constant juggle of patient care, motherhood, and self-care can feel overwhelming. But it's in this space of mental awareness that every thought, every emotion, and every impulse becomes a guide through life's ambiguities.

A personal technique or practice I use to maintain my mental clarity amidst life's challenges is that I give myself grace and tell myself it's ok not to be ok. Many times, I would think it wasn't ok because a few times I would beat myself up, thinking I was crazy or foolish. For example, when I was in the Psychiatric ward, I thought I was losing my mind until I started to heal.

It really makes me feel like I have the power to control myself in the midst of any adversities, even when people counted me out, so that I may encounter my own strength and self-worth. I felt free! I feel like I got this! It was not easy for me, yes, I had to go through the process of feeling alone, but I had to pull myself together to help other people just like me.

In the words of Audre Lorde, "Caring for myself is not self-indulgence, it is self-preservation, and that is an act of political warfare." Embrace this truth as you cultivate your mental awareness.

For Black women, especially those of us living with HIV, self-care is indeed a revolutionary act.

Unveiling Truth: Living with HIV - From Stigma to Strength

Living with HIV is not merely a medical condition; it is a crucible that challenges the depth of resilience and the breadth of empathy within the human soul. As a Black woman living with HIV, I've faced not just the physical challenges of the condition but also the weight of societal stigma and prejudice.

The statistics are sobering. According to the CDC, Black women accounted for 57% of new HIV diagnoses among women in the United States in 2020, despite making up only 13% of the female population. But we are more than numbers.

We are warriors, survivors, and thrivers. No matter what society says, we should never be afraid to live in our truth.

Your diagnosis is not your destiny. It's not a finale but an interlude that prompts a recalibration of life's melody. Every day, with the same hands that tenderly care for others, we weave a shield of resilience and advocate for recognition.

A moment of triumph over stigma and my diagnosis: I turned Prayer into a source of strength because at the end of the day, I knew my higher power was the only one that could pull me through this storm that was in my life. I didn't understand it, tried to figure it out, I couldn't.

I had to let go and give it to God. When I finally healed and accepted my diagnosis, I saw how my family, friends and community love me for me. Nothing people may not bless, but I use my experience to be a blessing to other people and to let them know they have a friend in me. Nobody judged me but they embraced me with love.

I used my diagnosis to help break the stigma and to help break the silence for many others who are afraid to use their voice. Ashamed to be living with HIV because stigma is still real. I raise awareness now to let others know we who are living with HIV can live a normal and healthy life because HIV is not a death sentence and be on proper medication to take care of ourselves. U=U means Undetectable and untransmissible.

We can't transmit the virus if we are Undetectable. HIV is not a crime even though people think it's a crime. We who are HIV Positive can love whoever we want, have children. Education is the key. The true fear is not knowing your status. We are quick to point the finger but not even know our own status.

As Zora Neale Hurston said, "There are years that ask questions and years that answer." Let this be your year of answers, of strength, of breaking free from the chains of stigma.

Reclaiming Self: The Mirror of Truth and Triumph

In the sanctuary of self-reflection, we confront the essence of our worth. As a woman who has weathered life's storms, I know that the anthem of worthiness has not always been a familiar refrain. It's often drowned out by societal expectations and internalized criticisms.

But hear me clearly: your worth is inherent, undeniable, and etched into the very fabric of your being. It's not determined by your health status, your relationship status, or society's narrow definitions of success.

I had to first love myself and accept everything about myself before I can love anyone else. It was "acceptance" I had to do, and live totally free. A lot of times we live in guilt and shame, that was me until I let everything go and started living for me and my family. I looked in the mirror and told myself I am somebody, I am a Black Beautiful Woman living my truth. I cry but I don't stay there.

Every day is not easy, but every day has been worth it, even the challenges I face, it was working for my good. I just had to believe that within myself. Everyone else could see it but I had to see it for myself. I was holding onto past hurt and not breaking free to what was holding me hostage. I wanted to scream for many days but I felt nobody was hearing me.

Thoughts were going through my head if I killed myself, I wouldn't have to face these different challenges, but when I finally healed and loved myself, it was like I finally saw the light. I saw whatever else would destroy me. I had to encourage myself when nobody else was there; I had to even pat myself on the back. When I felt alone, I had to tell myself, "You're not alone. You can do this". It was then I regained my strength and my power. I took back everything that tried to destroy me and turned it around into something powerful.

The weight that I used to carry on my shoulders I am able to unload and not pick it back up. Not knowing my own worth, I was very vulnerable and believed anything anyone would say to me. I had to pull out the good within me even when I didn't believe in myself.

The journey was not easy, many crying days but I had the willpower and determination to keep pressing. Nobody knows you but yourself. Anyone can say what they want to say about you but you don't have to answer to everything they say. As long as you know yourself, that is all that matters. I tell everyone you know yourself and we should never allow anyone to define us or our purpose.

We don't move forward and stay stuck because of what others say about us. I was like that one time until I stopped allowing people to define me. I healed and began to love myself all over again.

Remember Toni Morrison's words: "You are your best thing." Let this be your daily affirmation as you stand in your truth and reclaim your narrative.

Nurturing Growth: Blossoming Beyond Life's Thorny Paths

Growth often takes root in the richest of soils, born from the decay of past trials. As a single mother and healer of wounds, I embody both gardener and blossom. The fertility of our aspirations is nurtured not by remaining tethered to shadowy grounds but by reaching skyward.

Cultivating your inner garden requires a gentle touch, patience, and recognition that each seed of potential carries the blueprint of future greatness. It's a rhythmic practice of giving and taking, mastering the delicate balance of self-care and unwavering commitment to those we cherish.

When I became an advocate and motivational speaker, I felt really good about myself because I knew I was helping other people try to overcome whatever they were facing by sharing my personal experience in life. I educated myself about HIV Awareness and the laws, because the laws are not set up for those living with HIV. I was able to tell people living with HIV don't be afraid to disclose your status.

I am able to now travel across the world, even doing documentaries about my life with HIV. People will support you, and we who are living with HIV we should never be afraid to sit right at the table. It feels good to sit at the table; it shows me I got my power back, my strength, my voice. I feel really good helping many people who were just like me because I remember those dark moments in my life. I remember when I didn't know if I was coming or going. It feels good to know I'm making it. I know if I can make it many other people can too, you just have to believe in yourself.

Alice Walker reminds us, "And so our mothers and grandmothers have, more often than not, anonymously, handed on the creative spark, the seed of the flower they themselves never hoped to see." We are that flower, blooming against all odds.

Resilience Unchained: The Journey Continues

Our journey from sickness to social triumph is one of solidarity, not solitude. With compassionate hands, we extend beyond our narratives, touching hearts and shifting perspectives, transforming the stigma of our conditions into a resounding call for empathy and understanding.

As we traverse this path, our footsteps echo as a rhythm of empowerment, resonating in policy-making halls and quiet corners where silent battles rage. Our stories weave through society, changing hearts and aligning minds toward a future where sickness is no longer a shackle, but a shared human experience that evokes compassion and unity.

I started my own non-profit for HIV Awareness, wrote a book and even did a film. What motivated me was that I wanted to give back because I saw what stigma can do and how it feels to not have support, so I wanted to be able to help others through my organization, book, and film. This journey has made me stronger each day. I enjoyed seeing others smiling because they thought there was never hope. Seeing them smile again, knowing they were broken, hurt, confused and alone. Knowing they felt alone makes me feel good knowing I'm living the life I thought my situation was going to take me out of, but I am here to share my story with many people.

As we conclude this chapter, remember Nikki Giovanni's words: "Mistakes are a fact of life. It is the response to error that counts." Our resilience, our triumph over adversity, is not just a personal victory—it's a beacon of hope for all who follow.

A Moment for Reflection

Before we move on, I invite you to pause and reflect. Close your eyes and take a deep breath. Visualize yourself as a mighty tree, your roots deep in the earth of your experiences, your branches reaching towards the sky of your potential. With each breath, feel your strength growing, your resilience building. You are strong. You are worthy. You are unchained. You are a Beautiful Black Queen with a purpose for your life. You are stronger than you think.

As we turn the page to the next chapter, carry this image with you. The stories that follow will introduce you to more champions, more paths to resilience. Each narrative is a thread in the grand tapestry of triumph that we, as Black women, as humans, are weaving together. Let your heart be open to the wisdom they offer, and remember—your story, too, is an essential part of this masterpiece.

Porsha Vidaurre

TENDER HEARTS, STRONG SPIRITS

Overcoming Painful Pasts to
Embrace Bright Futures

7

TENDER HEARTS, STRONG SPIRITS

OVERCOMING PAINFUL PASTS TO EMBRACE BRIGHT FUTURES

By: Porsha Vidaurre

To create a safe environment, both physically and emotionally in order to thrive. Creating a safe space, both physically and emotionally, is essential for healing and thriving after trauma. With faith, resilience, and the courage to rest and rise again, we can find strength in our vulnerability.

Through professional support and self-compassion, we are guided by God's grace, finding victory in our journey toward wholeness and personal growth.

Creating a Safe Environment for Thriving

In the heart's whisper-soft throb, there reverberates a power, a persistent hum of nascent possibilities that yearns to crescendo into an opera of tenacious soulfulness and spirited vitality.

The power lies in constructing a haven—a sacred ecosystem—where one's being can flourish unimpeded, a protective sphere where every breath fuels the resilient growth of our tender hearts and strong spirits.

This, dear sister, is the essence of our journey: generating a sanctuary within and without, so we can navigate the turbulent tides of life with an anchored self-assurance.

Our principle guides us: to create a safe environment, both physically and emotionally, is not just a goal—it's the very foundation of our healing and growth.

As we embark on this transformative path, remember that your faith, your resilience, and your courage to both rest and rise again are the pillars of your strength. In the vulnerability of your healing, you will find a power that transcends the pain of your past.

Through professional support and the nurturing embrace of self-compassion, we open ourselves to God's grace, allowing it to guide us toward victory in our journey of wholeness and personal growth.

As you embrace these words, woven from the loom of hard-won wisdom, know that they are the building blocks of your fortress of empowerment.

With each paragraph, we lay down the stones of understanding, support, and personal enrichment, constructing an environment that fosters indisputable triumph.

Understand Trauma: Embracing the Past to Empower the Future

Sisters, let's get real about trauma. It's not just a word in some psychology textbook – it's the weight you've been carrying on your shoulders, the voice that whispers "you can't" when you're reaching for the stars. It's the legacy of generations before you, the expectations that don't quite fit, the dreams that seem just out of reach.

Society often emphasizes the importance of growing up in a two-parent household to instill family values and guidance. Unfortunately, my life has been far from that norm. From a young age, I experienced the instability of living in women's shelters with my mother and siblings, and by age 10, my siblings and I were split apart.

We lived with different family members after losing our mother in 1991. By the age 13, I was placed into foster care for three months.

I returned home, and by the age of 15, my siblings and I were placed into foster care permanently until we graduated from high school. Despite the hardships I endured, I refused to let them define me or hold me back. Even without my parents in my life I wanted to make both them and I proud. So I committed to furthering my education.

By staying focused, attending class, completing my homework, studying, and seeking help when needed, I became the first in my family to graduate from college, proving that adversity can fuel strength.

But hear me when I say this: your trauma does not define you. It is not your destiny. It is the springboard from which you will launch yourself into greatness. Every sleepless night, every moment of doubt, every tear you've shed in silence – these are not your weaknesses. They are the testament to your strength, the proof of your resilience.

As the incomparable Audre Lorde said, "I am not free while any woman is unfree, even when her shackles are very different from my own." Your healing isn't just about you – it's a revolution, a declaration of freedom for every sister who's walking in your footsteps.

Healing Through Professional Support: Embracing Guidance on the Path to Renewal

Listen up, goddesses! Self-care isn't just bubble baths and face masks (though if that's your jam, do you!). It's about building an unshakeable foundation of self-love and respect. It's about looking in the mirror every day and saying, "I am worthy. I am powerful. I am unstoppable."

Your coping mechanisms are your superpowers. Maybe it's pouring your heart out in a journal, letting your pen be the wand that transforms pain into power. Or perhaps it's losing yourself in the words of our literary queens – Michelle Obama's "Becoming," Shonda Rhimes' "Year of Yes." Let their stories fuel your fire!

Going to therapy is and was a crucial part of my self-care. It helps me address my emotional and mental well-being by giving me the tools to manage stress, navigate difficult feelings, and grow as a person. By prioritizing my mental health, I'm actively taking steps to create balance in my life and build resilience.

Building resilience isn't about never falling – it's about rising every single time, stronger and more determined. You come from a lineage of warriors, of women who turned pain into purpose and obstacles into opportunities. Their strength courses through your veins. Their triumphs are the prologue to your success story.

Surround yourself with people who see the queen in you, even when your crown is tilted. Seek out mentors who look like you, who've walked your path and can guide you through the thorns towards your roses. And always, always remember the words of the iconic Issa Rae: "I'm rooting for everybody Black." We're rooting for you, sister. Now it's time to root for yourself with that same fierce, unapologetic love!

Reclaiming Identity: The Journey from the Shadows into the Light

Queens, it's time to step into your light! Reclaiming your identity isn't just about knowing who you are – it's about shouting it from the rooftops, letting your brilliance blind the doubters and the haters. It's about embracing every curl on your head, every curve of your body, every dream in your heart.

After my mother passed, I went to live with my father in the country. During the mid-90s, I was one of the two African Americans in my class. In the city, they celebrated the late Dr. Martin Luther King's birthday by having the day off from school and work. In the country, they did not, and I couldn't understand why. I decided not to go to school as well. I'm not suggesting for anyone else to skip school by any means.

The point is that I understood the important role that Dr. Martin Luther King played not only in the African American community, but the world.

When I returned to school the next day, I was asked, "Why were you absent?" My response was to celebrate Dr. Martin Luther King Day. The administrator told me we do not consider that a holiday and handed me an unexcused mark for the day. I may have taken a mark for not being in school, but I left a bigger mark on my heart by standing up for Dr. King, my culture, and what I believe in: equality!

You're not just writing your story; you're rewriting the narrative for every black girl who's been told she's "too much" or "not enough." As the first in your family to snatch that college degree, you're not just opening doors – you're kicking them down for your siblings, your community, for generations to come.

Remember, your identity isn't carved in stone – it's a masterpiece you paint every day with bold strokes of courage and vibrant colors of self-love. You're not just a survivor, you're a phoenix rising from the ashes, ready to set the world on fire with your passion and purpose.

Roots and Wings: Building a Legacy While Soaring to New Heights

Listen up, sky-walker! You've got roots that run deep and wings ready to touch the stars. Your roots – the richness of your culture, the strength of your family, the power of your experiences – they're not anchors holding you down. They're the launchpad for your dreams!

Building a legacy isn't about having your name in lights (though if that's your goal, shine on, sister!). It's about lifting as you climb, about turning your trials into triumphs that light the way for others. It's about facing your fears with the fierceness of Sheba and the grace of a queen.

Growing up in a world of uncertainty and challenges shaped me in ways I couldn't always understand as a child. But now, those very trials have ignited a deep passion within me to reach back and uplift our youth and young adults. I want to be the nurturing, courageous voice that I once needed—someone to remind them that they are seen, heard, and capable of greatness. My dream is to inspire young hearts to rise as leaders in their homes and communities, to embrace love, and to chase their dreams boldly, no matter the obstacles life places in their path. Because every young person deserves to know they can overcome and thrive.

As you spread those wings and prepare for flight, keep Oprah's words close to your heart: "Think like a queen. A queen is not afraid to fail. Failure is another stepping stone to greatness." So go ahead, take that leap. The sky isn't the limit – it's just the beginning!

Embers of Hope: Illuminating the Darkness to Forge a Path of Light

Beautiful warriors, as we close this chapter, know that you are the embodiment of hope. Your tender heart isn't weakness – it's a wellspring of compassion that this world desperately needs. Your strong spirit isn't just for your own battles – it's a beacon for others still finding their way.

Healing isn't a destination with a neat little bow at the end. It's a journey, a dance, sometimes a wrestle. Embrace every step, celebrate every victory – yes, even the ones that seem small. Because every time you choose yourself, every time you rise despite the weight, you're lighting the way for someone else.

Toni Morrison said, "You are your best thing." So I'm telling you now: Believe in yourself with the ferocity of a lioness. Invest in yourself with the wisdom of an ancestor. Love yourself with the depth of an ocean and the height of the sky.

As we turn the page to the next chapter, remember this: Your future isn't just bright – it's blindingly brilliant. Your potential isn't just great – it's cosmic. The world isn't just waiting for you – it's holding its breath in anticipation of the gifts only you can bring.

Let God lead the way. Boldly stand, share your pain and defeat it. Step into the next chapter of your journey with your head high, your heart open, and your spirit unbreakable. Because, my sister, the stage is set, the spotlight is on, and it's your time to shine!

As we approach the threshold of a new chapter in our narrative, let us carry the embers of hope across the bridge to tomorrow. We venture forward, not in the absence of darkness, but with the knowledge that our inner light is enough to set the skies aflame with the brilliance of our purpose. Onward we go, towards a realm adorned with jewels of wisdom, self-love, and healing—a realm where our tender hearts and strong spirits are celebrated, cherished, and forever unbound.

Marsha Ford

DROPPING JEWELS

The Power of Faith, Self-Love and Healing

8

DROPPING JEWELS

THE POWER OF FAITH, SELF-LOVE AND HEALING

By: Marsha Ford

Marsha Ford is a spiritual mentor who combines traditional African-American wisdom with personal development principles to guide women in maintaining faith through life's challenges. Serving as a beacon of hope in her community, she teaches others to overcome obstacles by staying steadfast in their belief in the Most High.

As a survivor who rebuilt her life through faith and determination, Marsha's story inspires others to embrace their journey of healing and transformation. Connect with Marsha @MarshaFord on Facebook.com

Faith as a Pathway to Freedom

Reclaiming Power at Life's Crossroads

Sisters of the struggle, daughters of resilience, hear my call! I, Marsha Ford, come to you not just as a woman, but as a living testament to the power of faith, self-love, and healing.

The jewels I'm about to drop aren't mere adornments; they're hard-won wisdom from my own battles, forged in the fires of adversity and polished by the hands of divine grace.

From the urban landscapes where our dreams take root to the sacred spaces of our homes where we nurture the next generation, our journey has been one of faith, fierce love, and unyielding strength.

Right now, we're at a turning point, not just in our own lives, but in the big story of our people's history.

Let me tell my truth, for in vulnerability lies our collective power. At the age of 46, just after giving birth to my child through a C-section, I faced a crisis that shook me to my core. On my husband's birthday, after 20 years of marriage, I discovered pornography and phone numbers of other women on his phone.

The betrayal cut deep, not just into my heart, but into the legacy of love our foremothers fought to secure for us.

At that moment everything that I went through in my life flashed before me and the rose colored glasses were knocked off.

The illusion that I was living in disappeared in a blink of an eye. There was no denying the fact that I was manipulated not only by him but numerous others.

Miriam Makeba once said, "I will fight for the right of Africans to vote until I die." Sisters, I say to you now: I will fight for our right to love, to heal, and to thrive until my last breath.

Our struggle is not just personal; it's political, it's spiritual, it's revolutionary.

Faith as the Foundation

Finding Strength to Pursue Greatness

Listen closely, for I'm about to break it down like Chaka Khan breaks down a melody. Faith isn't some passive, Sunday morning accessory. It's the fire that fueled me when I decided to confront my reality and choose a path of self-respect and dignity.

When I faced the truth of my situation, faith wasn't just my comfort; it was my battle plan. I embarked on a thirty-day fast, a spiritual hunger strike against the forces of darkness that had invaded my home and my heart. And let me tell you, what the Lord revealed during that time was more nourishing than any earthly comfort could ever be.

Affirmation: "My faith is the vibranium of my soul, unbreakable and all-powerful. It's the foundation of my empire, the source of my strength, and the catalyst for my liberation."

Audre Lorde reminds us, "When I dare to be powerful, to use my strength in the service of my vision, then it becomes less and less important whether I am afraid." Embrace that power, sisters. Your faith is not just your shield; it's your sword, cutting through the lies that have bound us for generations.

Call to Action: Take a moment right now to write down three ways your faith has been your strength. How can you amplify that strength in your current situation?

The Power of Self-Love

Connecting with God and His Promises

Now, let's talk revolution – the kind that starts in your own mirror. Self-love isn't some new-age fad; it's a radical act of resistance against a world that's tried to convince us we're not enough. It's reclaiming the beauty our ancestors celebrated before anyone told them it was something to be ashamed of.

I've been the strong Black woman, the backbone, the mule of the world. But listen to me now: that stereotype is a chain, not a crown. It took me years to realize that my worth wasn't tied to my productivity or my ability to endure hardship. True strength lies in loving yourself fiercely, unapologetically, with the passion of Beyoncé and the depth of Nina Simone.

The biggest moment for me to show myself self-love was when I removed myself from an abusive emotional marriage. I was married to a man who used his religion as a way to manipulate me emotionally, spiritually, psychologically, and financially. For example, if I wasn't with him sexually, he withheld finances to pay bills so that I could care for myself and my kids. The way I decided to show self-love was by making a decision to leave this toxic relationship because my children and I deserved better. I started praying daily, I did affirmations, I made a decision to educate myself, and make a journey of self-healing. Daily prayer and thinking positively at all times were my rituals.

Affirmation: "I am a queen, sculpted by divine hands, heir to a legacy of greatness. My self-love is an act of revolution, a beacon for my sisters, and a force for change in this world."

Zora Neale Hurston wrote, "I love myself when I am laughing, and then again when I am looking mean and impressive." Embrace all of you – the joy, the rage, the softness, the steel. It's all part of the masterpiece that is you.

Call to Action: Create a self-love ritual for yourself. It could be a daily affirmation, a weekly pampering session, or a monthly check-in with your goals and dreams. Make it sacred and non-negotiable.

Healing Through Service

Empowering Others by Sharing Your Journey

Now that you've tapped into your faith and embraced self-love, it's time to turn that internal revolution outward. Your story isn't just yours; it's a chapter in the ongoing saga of our people's liberation. When I share how I rose from the ashes of betrayal to reclaim my power, I'm not just talking; I'm testifying. I'm not just sharing; I'm shattering the silence that has kept us bound.

Sisters, there is a way out. There are resources you can leverage to get help and protect yourself and your children in a safe way. By opening up about my experiences, I've been able to guide others towards the light at the end of the tunnel.

Affirmation: "My voice is a hammer, breaking the chains of silence. My story is a bridge, guiding my sisters from pain to power. In serving others, I serve the divine purpose written in my DNA."

Remember what Toni Morrison said: "The function of freedom is to free someone else." As you heal, as you grow, as you step into your power, you're not just changing your life – you're continuing the work of Harriet Tubman, Ida B. Wells, and every sister who dared to be free.

Call to Action: Reach out to a sister who might be struggling. Share your story, offer a listening ear, or connect her with resources. Your experience could be the lifeline she needs.

Rediscovering Your Authentic Self

Stepping Outside Your Comfort Zone

It's time to shed the masks, the code-switching, the "respectability" that's nothing more than oppression in disguise. Your authentic self isn't some hidden treasure; she's the warrior queen you've always been, waiting to roar.

I found the champion in me by embracing my roots, my voice, my vision. It meant downgrading in order to upgrade, living month-to-month to support my children while using my resources to build a better future. It's not easy, but neither was breaking free from a 20-year marriage built on illusions, and I didn't just survive – I thrived.

As a result of deciding to leave a 20-year marriage, I learned that I was looking for true love, and it was already within me.

Affirmation: "I am unapologetically Black, unapologetically woman, unapologetically me. My authenticity is my birthright, my power, and my gift to the world."

Beyoncé said, "I don't have to prove anything to anyone. I only have to follow my heart and concentrate on what I want to say to the world." Let that be your mantra as you step into your greatness.

Call to Action: Identify one aspect of your life where you've been dimming your light. Make a commitment to let that light shine, unfiltered and glorious, for the next week. Journal about the experience.

Breaking Generational Curses

Healing Trauma and Reclaiming Your Power

Now we're getting to the marrow, family. It's time to look at the patterns that have been passed down through generations – the acceptance of infidelity, the burden of silent suffering, the belief that we don't deserve true partnership. It's time to declare, "The buck stops here." You have the power to break chains that have held our people back for centuries.

When I confronted my husband and his child's mother, it became clear that this wasn't just about unfaithfulness – there was a spiritual attack at play. She revealed herself as a "reborn" demon, and in that moment, I knew I was in for the fight of my life. Breaking free meant reconnecting with the spiritual practices that have sustained our people through the Middle Passage and Jim Crow, through every trial and tribulation.

Affirmation: "I am the culmination of my ancestors' wildest dreams, the breaker of chains, the healer of generational wounds. My healing is an act of resistance, a balm for the past, and a blessing for the future."

Angela Davis reminds us, "I am no longer accepting the things I cannot change. I am changing the things I cannot accept." Let that be your battle cry as you face down generational curses and reclaim your birthright of joy, abundance, and freedom.

Call to Action: Identify one generational pattern in your life that no longer serves you. Create a ritual to release it – write it down and burn the paper, plant a seed to represent new growth, or create a piece of art that symbolizes your freedom from this pattern.

As we close this chapter, remember: you are not just the author of your story; you are the continuum of a legacy that stretches back to the cradle of civilization and forward into a future bright with possibility. The jewels I've dropped here are your birthright, your armor, your crown.

Know this: We were born to be queens, to rule not over others, but over our own destinies. There is light at the end of the tunnel, and that light is you – brilliant, beautiful, and bold. God put us here to be queens, and with the right partner, a queen is never belittled or made to feel less than.

In the words of the Quran, "Are those who know equal to those who know not? Indeed, they are not the same." You now know your worth, your power, your divine purpose. Step into it, sister. The world is waiting for your light.

Cynthia Holmes

BRUISED BUT BRAVE
Overcoming Adversity with Courage and Hope

9

BRUISED BUT BRAVE

OVERCOMING ADVERSITY
WITH COURAGE AND HOPE
By: Cynthia Holmes

Cynthia Renee Holmes is an educator, community advocate, and Founder/CEO of Holmes Helping Hands, Inc., a nonprofit empowering youth to overcome life's obstacles. Her journey through profound personal loss—having lost her entire immediate family—fuels her passion for the "Bruised But Brave" message of resilience. With two graduate degrees and recognition as School Employee of the Year (2022), Cynthia channels her experiences into creating pathways for others. She lives by her mantra: "Don't just give someone a fish; teach them to fish, and they'll eat for a lifetime—and perhaps become teachers themselves." You can connect with Cynthia at:

Holmeshelpinghands1@gmail.com

In life's symphony, every challenge is a somber note that, when played with resilience, creates a melody of strength.

Trials and Tribulations

The mirror reflects a face etched with experiences, eyes that have seen both darkness and light. This is the visage of a warrior, a Black woman who has walked through fire and emerged, not unscathed, but undefeated. The room around her is bathed in soft, golden light, a stark contrast to the shadows she's left behind.

In her hands, she holds a photograph, creased and worn from countless moments of reflection. It shows her family - her older sister, her two older brothers, and her mother. Their smiles freeze a moment in time, before loss and grief rewrote her story.

As she reflects back during her earlier years in life on how her older siblings would always make sure she received everything that she could have wanted, the tables slowly turned. All within 7 years, she lost all of her immediate family. Each death felt like a dream as she was walking in numbness so many times asking the Lord why me? Leaning and trusting in him for strength as there were days when there was a blur.

The air is thick with the scent of cocoa butter, a comforting aroma that speaks of heritage and home. It mingles with the faint smell of sage, burned to cleanse the space of negative energy. This is her sanctuary, a place where healing begins and strength is renewed.

She takes a deep breath, feeling the cool air fill her lungs. As she exhales, she lets go of the weight she's been carrying. The weight of an abusive marriage that not only distorted her self-image but also her very appearance. She remembers looking in the mirror and not recognizing herself, her face swollen, her spirit dimmed. But here she stands, bruised but brave, hurt but healing.

Affirmation: "I am not what happened to me. I am what I choose to become."

Quote: "The most common way people give up their power is by thinking they don't have any." - Alice Walker

Reflection: How have your trials, especially those involving loved ones, shaped you? In what ways have you reclaimed your power after abuse?

Takeaway: Our trials don't define us; they refine us. Even in the face of immense loss and pain, we have the power to redefine ourselves.

Standing Alone

Her gaze falls on a journal lying open on the bedside table. Its pages are filled with affirmations, each one a lifeline in moments of doubt:

"My wounds are where the light enters me." "I am the master of my fate, the captain of my soul."

These words, penned in moments of both despair and hope, serve as a testament to her resilience. They are her battle cry, her armor against the world's cruelty.

When the phone calls stopped on Sundays from her last sibling, the realization became so real. It was at that moment that she felt alone with no one to call anymore. Again, she was walking in a blur, asking herself who she could talk to, share ideas and programs to help children. Grits and Grandparents were replicated at her place of employment in honor of her last sibling.

If he was here to see the success, he would have been proud. Being a servant, helping others is the legacy that she shall carry on as her mother reached out to help many. Her doors were always open as she wanted the best for everybody.

She remembers the day she finally left her abusive marriage. The fear that gripped her heart, the uncertainty of the future. But also the undeniable knowing that staying would mean losing herself completely. Standing alone was terrifying, but necessary for survival.

On the wall hangs a vision board, a collage of dreams and aspirations. Images of strong Black women who've paved the way - Maya Angelou, Oprah Winfrey, Michelle Obama - are interspersed with quotes that speak to her soul:

"I am not free while any woman is unfree, even when her shackles are very different from my own." - Audre Lorde

Affirmation: "In solitude, I find my strength. In silence, I hear my truth."

Quote: "Caring for myself is not self-indulgence, it is self-preservation, and that is an act of political warfare." - Audre Lorde

Reflection: How has standing alone, especially after losing your entire family, helped you discover your inner strength? What have you learned about yourself in moments of solitude?

Takeaway: Solitude is not loneliness; it's an opportunity for self-discovery and growth. Embrace these moments to connect with your inner wisdom and rebuild your sense of self.

Finding My Way

She remembers the day she lost her older sister, her confidant. The world seemed to lose its color, sounds muffled as if she were underwater. She recalls the numbing pain, the feeling of being adrift in a sea of grief. But even in that moment, a small voice inside her whispered, "This too shall pass."

And pass it did, though not without leaving its mark. The loss of her older brother followed, each passing a fresh wound on her heart. In what felt like the blink of an eye, two pillars of her world had crumbled.

Then came the biggest blow - the loss of her dear mother. The unconditional love that had been her constant was now a memory. The pain was so deep, so all-encompassing, that she felt as if she might shatter into a million pieces. In the depths of her despair, she clung to the memories of her mother's love, a warmth that had always been her anchor.

Just when she thought she couldn't bear any more, life dealt its final, cruel blow. Her remaining older brother, the one closest to her in age, was taken from her. As the youngest of all her siblings, she had looked up to him, relied on his guidance and protection. With his passing, her entire immediate family was gone.

Standing alone in a world that suddenly felt too big, too empty, she found herself crying out to the universe, to God, to anyone who might listen: "WHY?" The question echoed in her mind, in her heart, in the hollow spaces where her loved ones used to be.

Why had she been left alone? Why had her entire family been taken from her?

In the silence that followed her anguished question, she felt the weight of her loss threatening to crush her.

Yet, even as she grappled with the enormity of her pain, she felt something else stirring within her - a resilience born from the love she had known, a strength forged in the crucible of her grief.

She realized that while she might never fully understand the 'why' of her loss, she could choose how to move forward. As the youngest, she now carried the legacy of her entire family. She could honor their memory by living with the love, strength, and resilience they had instilled in her.

Affirmation: "I carry the strength of my family within me. Their love guides me even in their absence. Though I may not understand why, I trust in my ability to move forward and honor their legacy."

Quote: "When you stand and share your story in an empowering way, your story will heal you and your story will heal somebody else." - Iyanla Vanzant

Reflection: As the youngest sibling, how has the loss of your entire family shaped your perspective on life and your role in carrying their legacy? In what ways have you found meaning in your struggles and honored their memory, even when questioning why it happened?

Takeaway: Our greatest pain can become our greatest purpose. Allow your experiences of loss to guide you towards your calling and to deepen your capacity for empathy and love. Even in the face of unanswerable questions, we can choose to move forward with purpose and grace, carrying the torch for those we've lost.

Perseverance and Endurance

She stands now, moving towards the window. The city outside is awakening, a symphony of car horns and distant voices. She sees herself reflected in the glass, superimposed over the urban landscape. In that moment, she realizes that she is not just a product of her environment or her past, but a force capable of shaping her future.

When life throws lemons, your faith and endurance can and will turn any situation into lemonade. As she is now the matriarch of the family, the glue to keeping the continuity of the family. She often reminds herself how she got to this point when everyone should be giving her direction, as she is giving support to her nephews and niece. The wall has to come down.

Her brother-in-law (oldest sister's husband) is still part of the glue, but there is work that needs to be done. As she continues to walk by faith, leaning on God and reminding herself that God has a plan that gives her the drive to keep pushing and walking in faith as he is ordering her steps. Her joy is seeing her children and grands become the fabric that they are made of "greatness."

Her hand reaches for her phone, opening the Therapy for Black Girls podcast. Dr. Joy's voice fills the room, a balm for her soul:

"Remember, healing is not linear. Some days you'll feel on top of the world, others you'll feel like you're starting from scratch. Both are okay. Both are part of the journey."

These words resonate deeply, reminding her that progress isn't always visible, but it's always happening. Even on days when grief feels fresh, when memories of her lost family members or the pain of her abusive marriage surface, she is still moving forward.

Affirmation: "I am resilient. I bend, but I do not break. The love of my family strengthens me even in their absence."

Quote: "You may encounter many defeats, but you must not be defeated." - Maya Angelou

Reflection: What keeps you going when times get tough, especially after experiencing such significant losses? How have you demonstrated perseverance in rebuilding your life?

Takeaway: Endurance is not about avoiding pain; it's about finding purpose in it. Your ability to persevere honors the memory of those you've lost and paves the way for a future they would be proud of.

Overcomer

She turns to her closet, selecting an outfit for the day. Each piece of clothing is a statement, an armor of sorts. As she dresses, she recites her daily affirmation:

"I am bruised but brave. I am hurt but healing. I carry the love of my lost family within me. I am, above all, hope incarnate."

Family is everything to her as she remembers on Sundays and holidays, coming together to feast and celebrate. It did not matter if you were near or far, it was a priority and now she has the mantle to keep it all together. Careers, life schedules and commitments often throw a wrench in her yearly plans, but she is optimistic that the celebrations will return. She continues walking in her purpose while honoring God's orders to continue being a servant while working through the ups and downs of having a non-profit, but with God all things are possible. One day her dreams of having a financially sound organization will become a reality.

With these words, she steps out into the world, ready to face whatever challenges may come. For she knows now that she is not just surviving, she is thriving. She is not just enduring, she is overcoming.

As she closes the door behind her, she pauses for a moment. The future stretches out before her, unknown but full of possibility. She takes a deep breath, squares her shoulders, and steps forward into her destiny. Though she walks alone physically, she feels the presence of her sister, brothers, and mother with her, their love a guiding force.

Affirmation: "I am not a victim of my history. I am a victor shaping my destiny, carrying the strength of my family with me."

Quote: "I am my ancestors' wildest dreams." - Unknown

Reflection: How has overcoming the loss of your entire family and the trauma of an abusive marriage prepared you for future challenges? What advice would you give to someone facing similar struggles?

Takeaway: You are not defined by what you've been through, but by how you've grown through it. Your story of overcoming is a beacon of hope for others who may be facing loss, abuse, or despair.

As we close this chapter, remember that your journey is far from over. In fact, it's just beginning. The trials you've faced, the solitude you've embraced, the way you've found through grief, the perseverance you've shown - all of these are preparing you for the next phase of your adventure.

In the words of Ntozake Shange, "I found god in myself & I loved her/ I loved her fiercely." As you step into the next chapter of your story, carry this truth with you. You are divine, you are powerful, you are love incarnate. The world is waiting for the brilliance of your fully realized self, shaped by the love of those you've lost and the strength you've found in overcoming.

Joyce Smith-Reid

THREADS OF TRIUMPH

Weaving the past into the Fabric of Future Success

10

THREADS OF TRIUMPH

WEAVING THE PAST INTO THE FABRIC OF FUTURE SUCCESS

By Joyce Smith-Reid

Joyce Smith-Reid's story is truly inspiring, especially her transformation from a law enforcement executive to a purpose-driven entrepreneur and CEO. With her background as a retired Chief Deputy, she's empowering women through her unique blend of resilience, truth, and self-worth. Her chapter, "Threads of Triumph: Weaving the Past into the Fabric of Future Success", is a powerful testament to embracing the lessons of the past to fuel a brighter future. And with Maya Angelou's words as a guiding light, Joyce embodies the strength to rise above challenges, reminding us all that while defeats may come, they don't have to define us. Stay up to date on the project and connect with Joyce by emailing **ladyjoy@sossolutionsllc.net**

My life is not just about resilience, it's about the choice to not be a statistic, the power to stand alone, and the ability to pull on a strength that has been suppressed time and time again.

The Weave of Resilience

In the intricate dance of life, resilience is the rhythm that keeps us moving forward. As an African American woman navigating the complexities of a world that often seems designed to hold us back, I've learned that resilience isn't just about bouncing back—it's about bouncing forward, higher and stronger than before. You realize that you can stand firm in the storm and be a beacon of tenacity.

Every experience is a thread that can lead to a legacy of excellence. This chapter is about resilience—not just surviving but choosing to thrive despite the challenges that seek to define us. It's about standing firm in the storms of life and weaving our past into a bright future filled with promise.

My journey began in a world where the odds were stacked against me. As a young professional in a male-dominated field, I found myself searching for a blueprint that didn't exist. I remember vividly the day I approached a senior commander, hoping for guidance and mentorship. Instead, I was dismissed without a second thought, shooed away like an unwelcome guest at a gathering I'd worked so hard to attend.

In the early part of my career, I was in a specialized unit, this unit offered everything I was looking forward to in my career. There was a balance of the exciting rush of the type of action you would see in police reality shows, taking down the bad guys and doing undercover work. Then there was the side that fed my love language of helping others through community engagement. I loved the intensity of it all. Then there was a side of law enforcement I had not thought about, nor was I prepared for.

I recall one assignment where we had to set up a perimeter to provide protection to a hate group while they protested outside of a county courthouse. It was the first time I had a racist comment hurled directly at me by one of the protestors. In my mind I kept trying to process the fact I had just been called a "monkey" and a "nigger bitch" and all I could think of was I could not lose focus, peoples lives could depend on it, including mine.

One day, I went to lunch with a colleague, and one of his relatives joined us. Once we arrived at the bistro, his relative stood up as we approached and asked, "who is this pretty little nigger girl you have with you?" He introduced me and pretended as if he had only heard a portion of what was said. Did I mention I was about seven months pregnant and doing all that I could to keep my blood pressure down?

Needless to say I wasn't hungry after all. In both incidents, I thought this couldn't be real. It was difficult to process the fact that I am here, in my protect and serve career field, an educated professional dealing with similar problems, my grandmother told us stories about from the 1950s and 60s. These types of stories were the reason she escaped living in Mississippi. I had always been courageous; this was just the beginning.

These moments could have shattered me. But instead, it ignited a fire within me. I realized then that if no support system existed for women who looked like me, I would become an architect. From that day forward, I committed myself to paving the way for others, ensuring that anyone who desired to join this "gathering" would be welcomed with open arms.

Resilience, I learned, is not a trait we're born with—it's a skill we cultivate through every trial we face. It's in the quiet moments of self-doubt, the sleepless nights worrying about our children's futures, and the daily microaggressions that we learn to navigate with grace and strength.

As Maya Angelou once said, "You may encounter many defeats, but you must not be defeated. In fact, it may be necessary to encounter the defeats, so you can know who you are, what you can rise from, and how you can still come out of it." These words have been a guiding light in my darkest moments, reminding me that each setback is an opportunity for growth.

Ancestral Strength

Our resilience as Black women is not just our own—it's a legacy passed down through generations. We stand on the shoulders of giants, women who faced unimaginable hardships yet persevered, carving out spaces for us in a world that tried to erase them.

I often think of my grandmother, a woman who was a sharecropper and cleaned houses to put her children through school, who talked to God like he was sitting on the couch next to her, her voice a testament to the unbreakable spirit of our people. Her hands, callused from years of labor, would gently smooth my hair as she told me stories of our ancestors—stories of struggle, yes, but also of triumph.

I look at my grandmother, Sadie Olivia Smith, and recall what she endured while working the fields in Mississippi and Arkansas and raising seven children. As an adult and a mother, I would wonder how she could have a relationship with God. Had he not let her down?

She still worked on old plantations, had a husband who would beat her just for GP (general purpose) and never had a driver's license. How could she be thankful for living this life in the hot, mosquito-infested town she lived in?

My mom, a teenage mother, left us to live with my grandmother often and I observed her strength up front daily. She finally got the strength to leave her husband after breaking her wrist with a wrench. She got her own house and began to come into her own.

I watched her grow from signing her name on insurance papers with an X to bartering goods from a local businessman to support the household. I knew she had it in her.

Most people could not pack up and leave everyone and everything they knew after traumatic incidents and start over in a new state. I had an upfront seat to strength and leadership, which would mold my life. James Louzes and Barry Posner define a leader as "an observable pattern of practices and behaviors, a definable set of skills and abilities".

It's this ancestral strength that flows through our veins, reminding us that we come from a lineage of survivors and thrivers. When I face challenges in my professional life or as a single mother, I draw upon this well of strength, knowing that I carry the hopes and dreams of those who came before me.

In the words of Audre Lorde, "I am not free while any woman is unfree, even when her shackles are very different from my own." This sentiment drives me to not only succeed for myself but to create pathways for other Black women to follow. Our individual triumphs are collective victories, each one a step towards a more equitable future.

Personal Trials & Triumphs

My life has been a series of trials that have forged me into the woman I am today. As a single mother working in a field where I was often the only Black face in the room, I've had to navigate waters that were not just unfamiliar but often hostile.

I was a police commander during the George Floyd incident and the city I policed in was not exempt from strife seen by the nation after this occurrence. After all, we had seen our own incidents in recent years which received national publicity, including the Walter Scott police shooting and the Emmanuel 9 mass church shooting. Both of these events shook the community to the core, a community I loved and thrived in.

As the protests began, I was appointed as the incident commander in a few of the demonstrations. Although I had trained for this prior to the election of President Obama, this one impacted me personally as it touched two areas of my life that I am passionate about, my police career and faith.

I knew the way to thrive through this was that I had always depended on my communication and connection with people. People could always see the mother, sister, aunt and daughter in me. I could use my "script" and collective experiences to get me through the tough conversations with the individuals representing the protestors.

In my reflections, I realized I had a script my whole life to get me through a number of tough times. These pathways of scripted communication produced a violence-free demonstration.

Each obstacle I've faced has been an opportunity to demonstrate not just my resilience, but my brilliance. I've learned to turn my differences into strengths, to use my unique perspective as a tool for innovation and problem-solving. I've found that resilience is not how you endure, it's how you recalibrate.

One of the most significant triumphs of my journey has been earning a Martin Luther King Trailblazer Award. This accomplishment wasn't just a personal victory—it was a statement to every Black girl who's been told she doesn't belong, that not only do we belong, but we excel.

As Shirley Chisholm once declared, "If they don't give you a seat at the table, bring a folding chair." I've taken this advice to heart, not just bringing my own chair but building new tables where all voices are heard and valued.

Weaving the Threads Together

The threads of our experiences—the trials, the triumphs, the moments of doubt, and the bursts of confidence—all come together to create the rich narrative of our lives. It's in the weaving of these threads that we find our true strength and purpose.

For me, this has meant embracing every aspect of my identity: my Blackness, my womanhood, my role as a mother, and my position as a leader in my field. It's meant recognizing that each of these facets adds depth and value to who I am and what I bring to the table.

One thing I realized in my time on this earth is that success will be accompanied by failure. I was in middle school, competing and winning in Odyssey of the Mind competitions, when our mobile home was repossessed. While in high school, I struggled in math but excelled in history and as a young college student, I became a wife and mother. In my career as a police officer, I struggled to find my identity, which was hard. Wearing male uniforms poses a multitude of challenges, making you feel alienated and also poor fit. I policed a community that did not embrace me in the beginning but only saw me as a traitor. Later in my career, I held titles as a "first in history of" on two different occasions. These could appear as a burden if you didn't decide to grab them as opportunities.

As a mother, I tried so often not to see my sons through the lens of a police officer. This made me extremely hard on them, and I put them in the context of statistics all the time. I don't have regrets, I have mirrors of reflection. Every time I looked at myself, I had to figure out how I was going to be a change agent for me, my family and my community. The answer was present in my past. My grandmother took many pieces of ugly patch fabric and sewed it into a beautiful quilt. The pieces of my life were the same, ugly patchwork thrown my way, yet my response made it a masterpiece.

As we continue on our journeys, it's crucial that we not only acknowledge our struggles but celebrate our victories, no matter how small they may seem. Each step forward is a triumph, each barrier broken is a path cleared for those who will follow.

Actionable Steps:

1. Reflect on your personal history. Identify moments of resilience and draw strength from them.
2. Connect with your cultural heritage. Seek out stories of ancestral strength and let them inspire you.
3. Set ambitious goals and create a plan to achieve them. Don't be afraid to be the first or the only—someone has to pave the way.
4. Find or create a support network of like-minded individuals who understand your experiences and can offer guidance and encouragement.
5. Practice self-care and self-compassion. Recognize that taking care of yourself is not selfish—it's necessary for your continued growth and success.

As we close this chapter and prepare to delve into the next, remember that your story is still being written. Every challenge you face, every victory you claim, is another thread in the beautiful, complex narrative of your life. The resilience you've cultivated, the strength you've inherited, and the triumphs you've achieved are all preparing you for the next phase of your journey.

In the words of Zora Neale Hurston, "There are years that ask questions and years that answer." As you move forward, be open to both the questions and the answers that life presents. Your experiences, your struggles, and your victories are not just your own—they are beacons of hope and inspiration for every Black woman fighting to make her mark on the world.

Embrace your power, honor your journey, and continue to weave your threads of triumph into the grand narrative of our collective success.

April L. Jacobs

UNQUENCHABLE SPIRIT

Rising From the Ashes of Pain to Empowerment

11

UNQUENCHABLE SPIRIT

RISING FROM THE ASHES OF PAIN TO EMPOWERMENT

By: April L. Jacobs

Embracing resilience is not just about enduring; it's about actively choosing to rise, heal, and reclaim my power, no matter how many times life has pushed me down.

The Ashes

Picture this: A young Black girl, hair in neat braids, stands before a cracked mirror. Her reflection is fragmented, much like her sense of self. But in her eyes, there's a spark – a glimmer of the queen she's destined to become. That girl was me, and this is our story.

"The greatest glory in living lies not in never falling, but in rising every time we fall" - Ralph Waldo Emerson

Sisters, have you ever felt the weight of these words in your bones? As Black women, our lives are a testament to this truth. We are the descendants of those who rose from the chains of slavery, who stood tall in the face of Jim Crow, who marched for our rights and continue to fight for our dignity.

I'm April Jacobs-Jones, and I'm here to tell you that your spirit is unquenchable. I've walked through the valley of abuse and trauma, felt the suffocating grip of anger and bitterness, and stared into the abyss of worthlessness. But I'm also living proof that you can rise from those ashes, your crown adjusted but unbroken, ready to reign.

I remember being at my lowest point. It was then that I decided to transform my life. After experiencing multiple domestic violent relationships, and dual sexual trauma, as well as battling years of low self-esteem and feelings of unworthiness, I decided to tap into my God-given resilience. I leaned into my faith, I prayed and asked God for guidance. I resolved to take accountability for not only the decisions I made, but also for my life.

Reflection: Take a moment to think about a time when you felt broken. Now, remember how you rose from that moment. What strength did you discover within yourself?

Overcoming Domestic Abuse Relationships

The day I left him, the air felt different. Thicker, charged with possibility and fear in equal measure. My hands trembled as I packed, each item a decision between past and future. Suddenly, a voice rose from deep within– clear, strong, and unmistakably mine. "April," it said, "you deserve better than this. You are worthy of love that doesn't hurt."

That voice was my lifeline, my North Star guiding me out the door and into a new life.

Sisters, if you're in an abusive relationship, I want you to hear that voice, too. You are not alone. According to the Institute for Women's Policy Research, more than 40% of Black women experience physical violence from an intimate partner during their lifetimes. But we are more than statistics. We are survivors, warriors, and healers.

The journey to leaving an abusive relationship is never an easy one. It certainly wasn't for me. I was 16 years old when I experienced the first physically abusive relationship. There were multiple domestically violent relationships that followed. These included: physical, emotional, mental, sexual abuse and financial abuse. With each abusive relationship, my self-esteem plummeted. While attending South Carolina State University, I experienced another physically abusive relationship, as well as sexual assault in 1993. After this experience, my grades dropped, and I was placed on Academic Probation. Instead of returning to SCSU after my probationary period was over, I decided to enlist in the U.S. Navy. This provided a new beginning for me.

Interactive Exercise: Write a letter to your younger self who experienced being in an abusive relationship. What would you tell her? What strength would you remind her she possesses?

Affirmation: "I am worthy of love, respect, and kindness. I choose to surround myself with people who recognize and honor my worth."

Breaking Free from Religiously Abusive Organizations

After my father's death, I was introduced to another religious organization. I made the radical decision to leave the Christian faith. I later realized the importance of not making major decisions while grieving. The religious organization that I became a part of went against many of the Christian values that were deeply embedded in me since my early childhood. Early in my involvement in this group, I married and had children. However, this was not a God ordained marriage to say the least. Polygamy was a common practice within this group, as well as living communally. Both of which I was in total opposition of. I accepted the fact that I was a part of a cult. After almost six years of marriage, and my husband taking a second wife, I decided enough was enough and I planned my "Great escape." With the support of family and friends, I was able to return to South Carolina with a bookbag, suitcase and my three babies in tow. It was quite a daunting task. I had to operate with a sense of strategy.

Discussion Question: How has your relationship with spirituality evolved over time? What practices or beliefs have you had to unlearn or reframe?

Overcoming Dual Sexual Trauma

This is hard to talk about, but it's important. I've experienced sexual trauma not once, but twice in my life. For years, I carried this pain in silence. I felt ashamed, dirty, and unworthy of love. But sisters, our silence doesn't protect us. It protects the systems and individuals that harm us.

According to the National Center on Violence Against Women in the Black Community, for every Black woman who reports rape, at least 15 do not report. We need to change this narrative. We need to speak our truth, loud and clear.

Healing from sexual trauma was met with many challenges, as well as breakthroughs. I experienced my second sexual assault shortly after my divorce. For years after this sexual assault, I felt blemished and dirty. I blamed myself and carried a great sense of anger, bitterness, and hurt. It was only after completely surrendering and rededicating my life to Christ. I also went through intense counseling. This brought me to the realization that who I am, nor whose I am is defined by my circumstances. As a result, I am here to tell you that regardless of the adversities and circumstances you face, you can rise to be all that God created you to be. You can soar like an eagle. I have since found a love that I prayed for. And I am happily remarried to a remarkable man.

Healing from sexual trauma is not linear. Some days you'll feel strong, other days the weight of your experiences might feel overwhelming. Both are okay. You're not broken. You're not damaged goods. You've gone from a victim to a thriver.

Healing Visualization: Close your eyes and imagine your body as a sacred temple. See the places where trauma has left its mark. Now, envision a warm, golden light slowly enveloping your body, healing and reclaiming each space. As you do this, repeat the affirmation: "My body is my own. I reclaim it with love, honor its resilience, and treat it with the tenderness it deserves."

The Road to Healing: Letting Go and Beginning Anew

Healing isn't a destination, it's a journey. For me, it began with forgiveness – not for the sake of those who hurt me, but for my own peace. It was about releasing the anger and bitterness that had become a poison in my soul.

As Audre Lorde said, "Caring for myself is not self-indulgence, it is self-preservation, and that is an act of political warfare." In a world that often tells Black women to put everyone else first, choosing yourself is a radical act.

Ritual for Readers: Consider creating your own ritual of release. What would you write down to let go? How would you symbolically release it? Share your ideas in a journal or with a trusted friend.

Affirmation: "I release what no longer serves me. I am open to new beginnings and the beautiful possibilities they bring."

Becoming Your Own Beacon: The Interplay of Self-Love and Boundary Setting

Imagine your life as a grand ballroom. In the center stands a magnificent chandelier – that's your self-love, illuminating everything around it. But what about the walls? Those are your boundaries, defining your space, protecting your light.

For too long, people came and went as they pleased, dimming my light, leaving muddy footprints on my soul. I learned to say no, to prioritize my needs, to choose myself – that was revolutionary.

Setting healthy boundaries was a difficult task for me. As a recovering people pleaser I struggled with saying no, as well as making myself a priority. I realized that setting boundaries is a vital part of self-care. I discovered this imperative fact while in counseling.

Dr. Thema Bryant, a Black psychologist and expert on trauma recovery, emphasizes the importance of boundaries in healing. She says, "Boundaries are a form of self-care. They are not selfish. They are necessary to protect your energy and your heart."

Self-Love Challenge: For the next week, start each day by looking in the mirror and giving yourself one genuine compliment. Notice how this small act begins to shift your self-perception over time.

Affirmation: "I am worthy of love, respect, and care – especially from myself. My boundaries are an expression of self-love."

Navigating the Voyage of Reclamation: Embracing Change and Cultivating Transformation

Change is inevitable, growth is optional. As Black women, we come from a long line of ancestors who embraced change as a pathway to freedom. Now, it's our turn to carry that torch.

For me, embracing change means planning to go back to school in my 50s to complete my degree in Social Work. It also means starting my own business to help other women heal from trauma. It meant being vulnerable and sharing my story, even when my voice shook.

Remember the words of Octavia Butler: "All that you touch, you change. All that you change, changes you." Embrace your power to create change, both within yourself and in the world around you.

Vision Board Activity: Create a vision board representing the life you're transforming into. Include images, quotes, and words that resonate with your journey of change and growth.

Affirmation: "I am the author of my own story. I have the power to create positive change in my life and in the world."

Sisters, we've traversed mountains and valleys in these pages, haven't we? We've confronted our pain, reclaimed our power, set our boundaries, and embraced change. But remember, this is just the opening chapter of your rebirth.

You're the protagonist in the greatest story ever told – yours. The pen is in your hand, the blank pages of your future spread before you. What will you write?

As you step into the next chapter of your life, carry these truths with you:

1. Your scars are proof of your healing, not your brokenness.
2. Your voice is a weapon, a lullaby, and a rally cry. Use it.
3. Self-love isn't selfish – it's revolutionary.
4. You have the power to rewrite any story that no longer serves you.

Go forth and shine, sister. The world is waiting for your light.

Affirmation: "I am powerful. I am resilient. I am worthy. I am enough."

Takeaways

As we close this chapter on our journey from pain to empowerment, let's reflect on the key lessons we've explored together. These takeaways are not just words on a page, sisters. They are seeds of transformation. Plant them in your heart, water them with your commitment, and watch as they grow into the beautiful, empowered life you deserve.

1. **Your resilience is your superpower:** You have weathered storms that would have broken others. This strength, this ability to rise again and again, is your birthright as a Black woman. Embrace it, celebrate it, and let it propel you forward.
2. **Healing is a journey, not a destination:** Be patient and kind to yourself along the way. Some days you'll feel like you're flying, others you might stumble. Both are part of the process. Honor wherever you are in your journey.
3. **Your voice is your power:** Speaking your truth, whether in a whisper or a roar, is an act of liberation. Your story has the power to heal you and inspire others. Don't let anyone silence you.
4. **Self-love is revolutionary:** In a world that often tells Black women to shrink, loving yourself fully and unapologetically is an act of rebellion. Make self-love a daily practice.
5. **Boundaries are acts of self-respect:** Setting and maintaining healthy boundaries is how you teach others to treat you. It's necessary for your wellbeing.
6. **You have the power to rewrite your story:** Your past experiences shape you, but they don't define you. At any moment, you can pick up the pen and start a new chapter.

7. **Community is crucial:** Surround yourself with people who reflect your value back to you. Seek out spaces where you can be authentically, unapologetically you.
8. **Your healing ripples out:** As you heal and grow, you create space for others to do the same. Your journey of empowerment has the potential to uplift your entire community.
9. **Embracing change is embracing growth:** Every challenge, every transition, is an opportunity for transformation. Don't fear change – welcome it as a catalyst for your evolution.
10. **You are worthy, just as you are:** Your worth is not determined by your productivity, your relationships, or your achievements. You are inherently valuable, simply because you exist.

Remember, sister, these takeaways are not the end of your journey – they're just the beginning. Use them as a compass as you continue to navigate your path of healing and empowerment. You've got this, and we've got you.

Reflections and Takeaways

1. What areas of your life are calling for healing and transformation?
2. How can you practice self-love and set healthy boundaries in your daily life?
3. What changes do you need to embrace to step into your full potential?
4. How can you use your voice and story to empower yourself and others?
5. What affirmations resonate with you, and how can you incorporate them into your daily routine?

1. In my journey, I found that journaling was a powerful tool for reflection and growth. While journaling I incorporate things that I am grateful for.

2. Therapy has also been an extremely powerful tool for me. Unfortunately, in our community and culture we often stray away from counseling.
3. **Community Share:** Consider sharing one of your reflections or takeaways on social media using the hashtag #UnquenchableSpirit. Your words might be the lighthouse another sister needs to find her way home.
4. As we close this chapter on rising from pain to empowerment, we open the door to new possibilities. In the next chapter, we'll explore how to harness your newfound strength and resilience to create the life you've always dreamed of. We'll dive into practical strategies for goal-setting, overcoming obstacles, and manifesting your desires.
5. Remember, sister, your transformation doesn't end here – it's only just beginning. The phoenix has risen from the ashes. Now, it's time to soar.

Angel Diggs

RISE AND SHINE

Finding Strength and Meaning in Life's Challenges

12

RISE AND SHINE

FINDING STRENGTH AND MEANING IN LIFE'S CHALLENGES

By: Angel Diggs

A. Diggs (Angel), known professionally as ADIGGS THECOACH, is a mental health advocate and life coach who transformed her own journey from teenage struggles to empowered leadership. In her chapter "Rise and Shine," she shares raw insights about resilience, drawing from her experiences as a young mother who refused to let circumstances define her destiny. As the host of the "AskTheCoach" podcast and a counselor dedicated to holistic wellness, Angel creates safe spaces for healing and transformation, living her message that "there is light at the end of each road when you are courageous enough to keep walking." Connect with Angel at askthecoach21@gmail.com or visit her AskTheCoach Facebook page.

Resilience is not just about surviving adversity but about tapping into inner strength, clarity of purpose, and the mindset required to rise above trauma. It involves embracing the grit to keep going, uncovering your 'why,' and rejecting false narratives that hold you back, all while preparing to shine as the fullest version of yourself.

What is it going to take to be resilient?

Girl, let me tell you somethin' – resilience ain't just a pretty word folks throw around. It's the backbone of every Black woman who's ever stood tall in the face of a world that tries to push her down. You feel me? We're talking about that fire in your belly that keeps you moving when everything and everyone is telling you to quit.

I remember when I was just a young thing, barely 17, thinking the weight of the world was gonna crush me. Challenged with major responsibilities, while pushing to survive in a cruel world where everything that glitters is not gold, versus every friend you think is ten toes down will fold. Constantly watching my back because the streets were nothing nice, especially for someone like me. Having to sell drugs and more to make ends meet. I was fortunate to have both my parents living, however, my family did not protect me when I needed them the most due to them trying to take care of the household, leading to what I now know was a choice to face the world alone.

But here's the thing, sis – resilience is about more than just surviving. It's about thriving. It's about looking at every obstacle and saying, "Watch me climb this mountain in heels." It's about finding that inner strength that our ancestors passed down to us, generation after generation.

You know what Maya Angelou said? "You may encounter many defeats, but you must not be defeated. In fact, it may be necessary to encounter the defeats, so you can know who you are, what you can rise from, how you can still come out of it." That's the kind of resilience I'm talking about.

Affirmation: "I am the descendant of women who survived the unimaginable. Their strength flows through my veins."

How to get the grit and persistence to keep going?

Now, let's talk about grit. That's not just sand in your shoes; it's that rough, raw determination that keeps you pushing forward when you want to fall back. It's what gets you out of bed when the world feels too heavy, what makes you apply for that job one more time, what helps you face another day of microaggressions with your head held high.

While dealing with the challenges I mentioned earlier, I hit another fork in the road. I was at the point where I ran into another mountain in my path and had to figure out how to make it through this one. I was a pregnant teen with limited resources. Becoming a single mom was definitely not in my plans; however, I had to use my grit in which most will call determination, and make the decision that no matter what lies ahead, giving up is not an option. I had to make it for me and my baby. It was through these life situations in that I knew I had to push and push if I wanted to make big strides in what I needed to accomplish. I set goals as well as set boundaries and stuck to them no matter what. I had to hold myself accountable for my actions and thoughts.

Listen, the road ain't easy for us Black women. According to a study by the National Women's Law Center, Black women in the U.S. typically make only 63 cents for every dollar paid to white, non-Hispanic men. But we persist. We keep showing up, keep breaking barriers, keep proving our worth.

Remember what Shirley Chisholm said: "If they don't give you a seat at the table, bring a folding chair." That's the kind of persistence we need. We don't wait for opportunities; we create them.

Affirmation: "My persistence is my power. Every step forward is a victory."

Knowing Your 'Why'?

Now, let's get to the heart of it all – your 'why'. This is what keeps you going when everything else is telling you to stop. It's your purpose, your mission, your reason for getting up every single day.

For me, my 'why' is me. I had a number of why's in my life that I constantly felt the need to reevaluate. I've learned to reach my goal of helping my fellow strong women. I must stay true to my values by being an example while also uplifting others.

Your 'why' is personal. It's what speaks to your soul. Maybe it's your children, your community, your dreams of changing the world. Whatever it is, it needs to be strong enough to pull you through the toughest times.

As Oprah Winfrey said, "Create the highest, grandest vision possible for your life, because you become what you believe." Your 'why' is that vision, that belief in what you can become.

Reflection: Take a moment to write down your 'why'. What drives you? What would make all the struggle worth it?

Mindset is everything; Don't believe the lies

Now, let's talk about that beautiful mind of yours. Your mindset is the key to everything. It's the difference between seeing obstacles and seeing opportunities.

But girl, the lies! The lies the world tells us about who we are and what we're capable of. They'll have you believing you're not enough, that you don't belong, that you can't succeed. Don't you dare believe them!

In 2006, I was going through so much. I thought that I had nowhere to go, no one to talk to, and no one to help me. My mind was feeding me lies. All lies that were coming to me were pouring memories of my past experiences that had the ability to cripple me, make me continue to be in a state of no progression. Fearful of what was to come and what I had to leave behind. Thankfully that I was able to have access to positive mentors by this point who encouraged me, and I also tapped back into the reason for my pressing. I had to put into action my self-reflection, meditation, and affirmations. This helped me to get back on track to combat the negative talk and change my mindset to a more positive shift.

According to the American Psychological Association, Black women face unique stressors related to racial discrimination and gender bias. But here's the thing – we're not victims. We're warriors. We take those struggles and turn them into our strength.

As Audre Lorde said, "When I dare to be powerful, to use my strength in the service of my vision, then it becomes less and less important whether I am afraid." That's the mindset we need to cultivate.

Affirmation: "I reject the lies that limit me. My potential is limitless."

It's time to shine!

Alright, queen, it's your time to shine! You've done the work, you've faced the challenges, and you've persisted through it all. Now it's time to step into your light.

Shining isn't about being perfect. It's about being authentically, unapologetically you. It's about using your voice, sharing your story, and lifting others as you rise.

Let this be a guide, an inspiration, or motivation for you to know: YOU CAN MAKE IT SIS! Know that "there is light at the end of each road when you are courageous enough to keep walking". I know the importance of striving, the heartache and hurt of pushing through pain for a bigger purpose. Take this time out to celebrate your wins, big or small. You are worthy of all good things. It can be hard to celebrate you because you are used to celebrating others. I am here to remind you, YOU ARE WORTHY OF CELEBRATING TOO!

Remember, when you shine, you light the way for others. According to a study by McKinsey & Company, when women are represented in leadership roles, they're more likely to hire and promote other women. So your success isn't just about you – it's about all of us.

As Issa Rae said, "I'm rooting for everybody Black." And girl, we're rooting for you.

Affirmation: "I am ready to shine my light. My success inspires others to shine too."

Takeaways:

1. Resilience is your birthright – claim it.
2. Persistence is your superpower – use it.
3. Your 'why' is your compass – follow it.
4. Your mindset shapes your reality – choose wisely.
5. Your light is meant to shine – let it.

As we've explored the power of resilience, grit, and shining our light, we've seen how our inner strength can propel us from pain to empowerment. Now, as we turn the page to the next chapter of our journey, we'll discover how this newfound strength can help us navigate one of life's most challenging terrains - the landscape of love and faith. Get ready to explore how resilience plays a crucial role in healing broken hearts and reclaiming our faith, not just in others, but in ourselves and the divine plan for our lives.

Michelle Warren

BINDING THE BROKEN VOWS

Reclaiming Faith After Infidelity

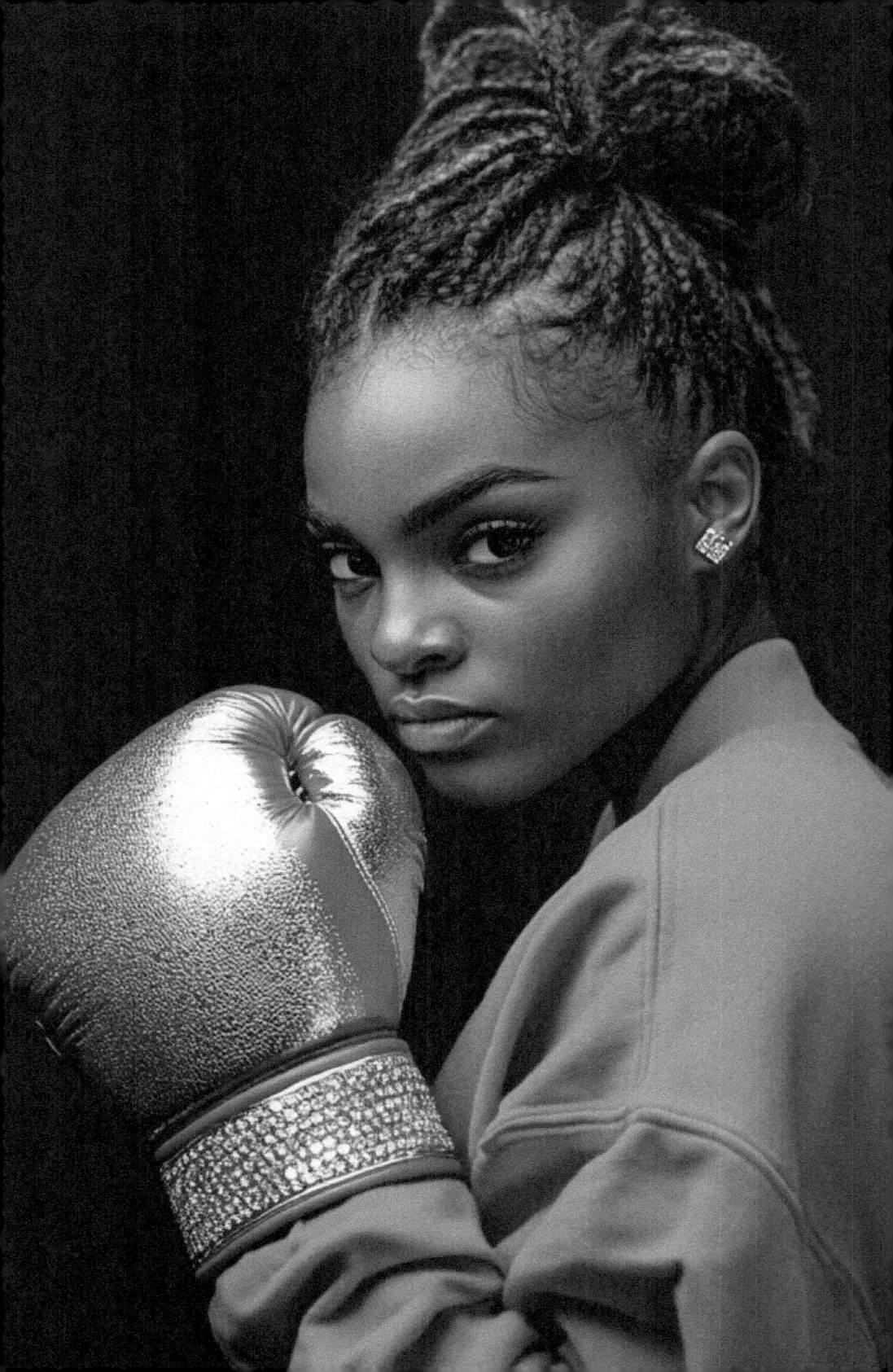

13

BINDING THE BROKEN VOWS

RECLAIMING FAITH AFTER INFIDELITY

By: Michelle Warren

Adultery does not have to lead to divorce. With courage, faith, and commitment, it can become a catalyst for personal growth, healing, and a stronger, more fulfilling marriage.

Queens, gather 'round and listen up! I'm about to speak some truth that's gonna shake your soul and lift your spirit. In the quiet corners of your heart, where the echoes of betrayal still linger, I want you to know that you're standing on holy ground. This isn't just a battlefield; it's your launching pad to greatness.

As a Black woman who's walked this fiery path, I know the weight of the pain you're carrying. I've felt the sting of betrayal cutting deep, threatening to shatter everything I believed about love and trust. But let me tell you something, sister - that pain? It's not your final destination. It's the cocoon from which you're about to emerge, stronger and more magnificent than ever.

In 2012, I had just married the man that I told all my friends in high school would be my husband one day and I was on cloud nine. Just 5 months into our marriage, I discovered that he had an affair. I saw footage that I could never get out of my mind. I knew my marriage was over. I WAS NOT the kind of girl who gets cheated on and my pride kicked up something serious. The level of anger, betrayal, and straight-up hatred (sorry to say it, but it's real) I felt was something I had never experienced before. It was a scene out of Waiting to Exhale, and I was Angela Bassett setting the car ablaze. My soul was crushed and it was a pain that I could not put into words. I knew I needed to PRAY because marriage is God's institution and not just a mere piece of paper or a contract with the government, but it was a covenant that was meant to be unbreakable.

Matthew 19:8 (NIV) Jesus replied, "Moses permitted you to divorce your wives because your hearts were hard. But it was not this way from the beginning."

I was led to that passage of scripture, and in spite of all the pain I felt, I remember this small, small and I mean SMALL, place inside of me wondering if this could be salvageable and if I would recognize myself if I stayed.

I took a few days off of work, grabbed my Bible and fasted for the first time in my life. Admittedly, I just wanted the peace I needed to help me exit the marriage, but in my time of seeking HIS way, I heard, "This is not about you and there is work to be done." It was a defining moment for me, and I had a choice to make - carry out my will or surrender to him. It was this moment that I knew this was a life-changing decision and the acceptance that I may not ever know this version of myself again and the possibility that what was on the other side was actually better. This doesn't mean I was instantly healed from the pain, matter of fact, far from it.

However, I knew that God was greater than what I was going through and that he could and would get use out of it in my life. It was a catalyst for me to lean into my faith and truly TRUST. It wasn't until my trust was shattered that God could come in and start putting together a new masterpiece. In that moment, I felt a surge of hope not just for us, but for the new ME.

Now, I want you to plant your feet firmly and declare with me: "I am not defined by what was done to me, but by how I rise above it." This is your moment to reclaim your power, your joy, and yes, even your marriage if that's what your heart is calling you to do.

Remember what the queen, Maya Angelou, said: "You may encounter many defeats, but you must not be defeated." Let these words be the war cry that ignites your soul as we embark on this journey of healing and reclaiming your faith.

It's Not Me, It's You - Nope, it's US Two!

Listen up, because this part is crucial. That voice in your head is trying to convince you that somehow this is your fault? It's lying to you. The choice to step outside the marriage wasn't yours. That decision, that betrayal, that's on them. Period. Full stop.

I know it's tempting to replay every moment, wondering what you could have done differently. But sis, it's time to change the record. You are a queen, forged in the fires of ancestral strength, with a legacy of resilience pumping through your veins. The actions of another do not define you. They do not dim your light. In fact, how you rise from this moment will only make you shine brighter.

Infidelity took place in my marriage more than once. I had to figure out who I was now independent of my partner. I was not just a wife, a mother, a sister, etc., who experienced betrayal. I found out that I am a force, a change agent, and an overcomer. I learned that while I am not responsible for another person's actions, I did have a part to play in the scenario and that is all I could and should focus on. What was it in ME that still needed work? It made no sense for me to rehash what his thoughts were and all the reasons why.

You have to fight the urge to think that you are the sole reason something so tragic has happened. Own your piece and own your peace! It was clear my husband had his own struggles that led to his decisions and I had my own that ignored some signs our marriage was in trouble, even in its early stages. What I had to lean into was that I was not a failure for what happened. In fact, maybe this was also a test to reveal where my relationship with God actually was and not what I pretended it to be.

I knew I needed help sorting through all the emotions and to look deep within myself for answers. I was referred to a coach to help me navigate this space. The coach's niche was focusing on wives who are standing in the gap for their husbands. In a conversation with her, she asked me if I had forgiven and prayed for the other woman and not just my husband. My eyes were like a deer in headlights, 'Say what now?! You want me to pray for the ops?!' She quietly asked a second time and reminded me that I professed to be a believer in Jesus Christ, so why was this a hard concept? Ouch! It was in this discussion that I realized that this was indeed so much bigger than my pain, but that in this situation, I had the opportunity to be a vessel for the work of God. Talk about a perspective shift!

It was in this that the definition of my self-worth changed and I started to see myself as truly valuable, not just in the flesh but in the spirit! Instead of thinking that this happened because I gained weight or maybe he doesn't think I am pretty, or whatever else the enemy would plant in my thoughts, I started to see the beauty in who God made me to be to even be receptive of this alternate vantage point. I still had no idea if my marriage would survive, but I knew that what I did have at my disposal was prayer and that made me aware of my greatest power.

Zora Neale Hurston once said, "I love myself when I am laughing, and then again when I am looking mean and impressive." Embrace every facet of yourself on this journey - the hurt, the anger, the hope. They're all valid, and they're all fuel for your transformation.

Affirmation: "I am whole, I am worthy, I am enough - with or without a partner."

Forgiveness is Your Superpower

Now, let's talk about the F-word that I touched on and makes everyone uncomfortable - Forgiveness. Before you even think about closing this book, hear me out. Forgiveness isn't about letting someone off the hook. It's not about saying what happened was okay. Forgiveness is your superpower, your secret weapon in this battle for your heart and soul.

When you forgive, you're not doing it for them - you're doing it for you. You're declaring, "I refuse to let this pain control my life any longer." It's like breaking out of a prison you didn't even realize you were in.

90 days into my separation, I was still struggling with this idea of forgiveness. I knew I needed to extend it, but I truly didn't know what that looked like and if it was synonymous with reconciliation. I learned it wasn't and that I had to forgive regardless of if I chose to work it out or not for the sake of my own life and future.

I would love to say that I just decided to do the right thing, but I didn't. The hurt was deep, sis. I found out I was pregnant at this point and was extremely conflicted. Out of my pain, I withheld that information from my husband for a period of time until I suffered a medical complication and had to tell him what was going on. We had a conversation and the words of my coach echoed in my mind. It wasn't because of the child that we HAD to reconcile or that I had to forgive, but it was only right. I had a moment of thinking that what I was carrying in my heart manifested in my body. My unborn child was suffering and on the ultrasound, it showed her in the womb, covered by "The Blood!" It was then that forgiveness jumped out at me. Trials come and go, we can be in pain, but there is a covering and that greatest covering offers us FORGIVENESS.

I don't know what it might be for you, but I know that something in your life will show you that you cannot move forward without it. For me, literally, it was life and death! Metaphorically, it is the same for you sis. Your life depends on it, the condition of your well-being and the future requires that you not harbor unforgiveness in your heart.

Colossians 3:12-14 (NIV) - "Therefore as God's chosen people, holy and dearly loved, clothe yourselves with compassion, kindness, humility, gentleness, and patience. Bear with each other and forgive one another if any of you has a grievance against someone. Forgive as the Lord forgave you. And over all these virtues put on love, which binds them all together in perfect unity."

Remember, forgiveness is a journey, not a destination. It's okay if it takes time. Be patient with yourself. As the wise Iyanla Vanzant says, "Forgiveness is a gift you give yourself." Claim that gift, sis. It's yours for the taking, and it's the key to your freedom.

Affirmation: "I choose forgiveness not because they deserve it, but because I deserve peace."

Faith is the Substance of Things Hoped For

In the eye of this storm, faith becomes your anchor, your lifeline, your North Star. It's what keeps you standing when everything around you is crumbling. Faith whispers to your soul that there's still hope, even when your eyes can't see it yet.

As Black women, we come from a long line of faith warriors. Our ancestors held onto hope in the face of unimaginable hardships. That same strength, that same unwavering faith, lives in you. It's time to tap into it, to let it rise up and carry you forward.

Faith isn't just about believing in God; it's about believing in yourself and the power of love to heal and transform. It's about trusting that this trial is not your final chapter, but a powerful plot twist that's setting you up for a glorious comeback.

When my husband came home to look after me and his unborn child, the moment I laid eyes on him, everything came rushing back. To be honest, it sent me into an emotional tail-spin that I was not fully prepared for or at least I thought I wasn't. The first few nights of us sharing a space again, I wept like a child in silence. My spirit said I could do this and my flesh said, "Girl, you're not ready." That feeling of being at war with myself was unsettling.

There was no evidence that my heart would be safe with him again, so all I could do is have faith. He told me he would fight for us, do better, try harder and his words weren't enough. Only what God's word could hold the fragments of my heart and give me hope in spite of my fears. Psalm 91:1-2 (NLT) "Those who live in the shelter of the Most High will find rest in the shadow of the Almighty. This I declare about the Lord; He alone is my refuge, my place of safety; he is my God, and I trust him."

The fact is that I realized my faith didn't have to be in my husband, but in God who made this institution of marriage. I remember telling God, that if this honors you then lead me through.

Let the words of Hebrews 11:1 light a fire in your spirit: "Faith is the substance of things hoped for, the evidence of things not seen." Your faith is creating a new reality, even now. Believe it, claim it, live it.

Affirmation: "My faith is stronger than my fears, and it's leading me to a future filled with love and joy."

Better than Ever: Beauty for Ashes

Now, queens, let's talk about the glow-up that's waiting on the other side of this valley. I'm not just talking about getting back to where you were before. I'm talking about building something so beautiful, so powerful, so fulfilling that your past self wouldn't even recognize you.

This journey of healing and rebuilding isn't just about saving a marriage. It's about personal transformation. It's about emerging from this fire refined, like gold, with a strength and wisdom that will leave people in awe.

My husband and I found a renewed sense of commitment, love, and respect for each other. This journey was not fast by any stretch of the imagination. The difference now is that we are so much better at communicating where we are, making sacrifices to meet each other's needs even when it's hard or not ideal, and being honest with each other. We were 27/28 year old kids who decided to get married, and every few years we were morphing into different people with different needs.

Unfortunately, infidelity was our teacher, but instead of letting it ruin us, we trusted God to rebuild the foundation. When we really looked at how God loves us and made a conscious decision to emulate that every chance we could, it catapulted our marriage into new heights.

When challenges arise now, we check in and are honest about where those feelings are leading us. We don't assume what the other is thinking, and our conversations are constructive, and we never tear each other down when expressing ourselves.

This marriage is not the marriage I had 13 years ago! I look at myself now, and I am glad that I do not recognize the old me or the old him. We talk about infidelity in our relationship and it is hard to imagine that it was really US that went through it! It feels like we are talking about a couple we once knew, and in some ways, we are.

The key is to truly let go. Let go of your expectations of how the healing will happen, how your spouse will change, and embrace the beauty that lies in the unknown.

Isaiah 61:3 promises "beauty for ashes, the oil of joy for mourning, the garment of praise for the spirit of heaviness." This isn't just a nice saying; it's a prophecy over your life. Claim it. Own it. Live it out loud.

Your story isn't over; it's just getting to the good part. You're not just healing; you're evolving into a version of yourself that's going to change the world.

As we close this chapter, I want you to hold onto this truth with everything you've got: You are capable of healing. Your marriage is capable of not just surviving, but thriving. The road ahead won't be easy, but baby, it will be worth it.

In the next chapter, we're going to dive into how to balance all the roles you play - wife, worker, wonder woman - while nurturing your healing journey. Because you're not just rebuilding a marriage; you're crafting a legacy of resilience and love that will inspire generations.

Remember, queen, you've got this. And I'm right here cheering you on every step of the way.

Kenya Cobb-Myers

WIFE, WORKER, WONDER WOMAN

Balancing Love, Career, and Resilience

14

WIFE, WORKER, WONDER WOMAN

BALANCING LOVE, CAREER, AND RESILIENCE

By: Kenya Cobb-Myers

Kenya Cobb-Myers is a multi-talented mompreneur, career woman, and devoted wife who knows firsthand the weight of wearing many hats. Driven to be a voice for women who give selflessly yet often go unappreciated, Kenya believes that love always wins and that life is a delicate balancing act. In her chapter on balancing love, career, and resilience, Kenya shares her journey and her guiding principle: treat others as you would want to be treated. Connect with Kenya on Instagram @all.things.love2

Balancing multiple roles requires intentional prioritization and self-compassion

Listen, sisters! It's time we had a heart-to-heart about this beautiful, chaotic juggling act we call life. You're the wife holding down the fort, the worker climbing that career ladder, and the wonder woman keeping it all together. I see you, I feel you, and I'm here to tell you that you're not alone in this whirlwind of responsibilities.

As an employee, a mother, and a wife, I've walked in those stilettos you're wearing. I've felt the pull in every direction, the weight of expectations, and the burning desire to excel in every role. But let me drop some hard-earned wisdom on you: it's not about being perfect in every role, it's about being intentional with your priorities and showing yourself some much-needed compassion along the way.

There was a time when I was juggling more than I thought I could handle. I was deep into a critical project at work, with looming deadlines that demanded late nights and early mornings. At the same time, my 6-year-old had a liberal arts production coming up, something he'd been excited about for weeks, and my 8-month-old was going through a rough teething phase that left me drained and sleep-deprived. On top of that, household responsibilities and being present in my marriage weighed heavily on me. It felt like there was never enough time to give everyone and everything the attention they deserved.

I found myself trying to do it all—staying up late to finish work, waking early to get my kids ready for the day, trying to be the perfect mother, wife, and employee. I was running on empty. That's when I realized something had to change. I couldn't pour from an empty cup, and striving to meet every expectation perfectly was only leading me to burnout.

It was then that I embraced the principle of intentional prioritization. I sat down and asked myself what truly mattered at that moment. I realized that work was important, but so was my son's school performance and being emotionally available for my family. I also recognized that I needed to take care of myself if I was going to be present for those I loved. It became clear that I had to let go of trying to achieve everything perfectly.

So, I made some adjustments. I communicated with my boss and team about my workload, delegating tasks and setting realistic deadlines that allowed me to breathe. I focused on the work that truly needed my attention and let go of the smaller tasks that could wait. At home, I gave myself permission to not be the "perfect" mommy. I ordered takeout for dinner instead of stressing over cooking, and I made sure to carve out time to rest—even if it was just 20 minutes to close my eyes or enjoy a hot latte.

On the night of my son's performance, I sat in the audience, fully present, without worrying about the mountain of work waiting for me. At that moment, I was where I needed to be. My son's beaming face, knowing I was there cheering him on, reminded me why prioritization matters. I was intentional about focusing on what was most important in that season of my life—my family and my own well-being.

Throughout this journey, self-compassion became essential. I learned to embrace imperfection and recognize that doing my best is enough. Some days, the house was messy, and tasks took longer than expected, but I realized that balance comes from making intentional choices and being kind to myself.

This experience emphasized the importance of prioritizing what truly matters and deepened my spiritual understanding of self-compassion. By releasing unrealistic expectations and allowing myself to rest, I became more present, effective, and at peace in navigating my many roles.

You see, I learned the hard way that trying to be everything to everyone all the time is a recipe for burnout. It took me hitting a wall to realize that balance isn't about giving 100% to everything all the time. It's about consciously deciding what needs your attention most at any given moment, and being okay with letting some balls drop occasionally.

Balancing Roles: The Juggling Act

Imagine this: It's 6 AM, and you're already up, prepping everything for the kids, reviewing that presentation for work, and mentally going through your to-do list. Sound familiar? That's the life of a Wife, Worker, Wonder Woman. It's a delicate dance, and sometimes it feels like you're doing it in heels on a tightrope.

But here's the thing – this juggling act? It's where your strength shines. Each ball you keep in the air is a testament to your resilience, your love, and your determination. It's not about doing it all perfectly; it's about doing it all with purpose and intention.

As a spiritual woman, wife, mother, and career professional, I understand the importance of balancing my external responsibilities with my internal well-being. The "Three MITs" strategy (Most Important Tasks), rooted in spirituality, helps me stay grounded and aligned with my values.

This strategy, rooted in spirituality, helps me stay grounded and aligned with my values. For instance, I begin my day with a quiet moment of prayer or reflection, seeking guidance on how to approach the day with purpose and love. I then identify my Most Important Tasks (MITs), which typically encompass spiritual, work-related, and family-related priorities.

By incorporating spirituality into the "Three MITs" strategy, you're not only managing your time effectively but also grounding yourself in something deeper. This helps you approach your day with a sense of purpose and connection, making it easier to navigate challenges with clarity and calm.

Affirmation: "I am the master of my many roles. With each hat I wear, I bring love, strength, and purpose. I prioritize with intention and treat myself with compassion."

The Power of Partnership: Being a Supportive Spouse

Now, let's talk about that partnership you're nurturing at home. Marriage isn't just about love; it's about teamwork. It's about having each other's backs when the world feels like it's coming at you from all sides.

In my house, we live by the motto: "We got this." It's not just about me winning or him winning; it's about us winning together. When my husband succeeds, I succeed. When I thrive, he thrives. That's the power of true partnership.

My husband and I rely on a practice we call the Weekly Check-In & Planning Session to maintain a strong and supportive relationship, especially when juggling work, parenting, and household responsibilities. This simple yet powerful strategy keeps us aligned and ensures we remain a united team through all the demands of life by setting dedicated time to discuss the week ahead, share schedules, coordinate responsibilities, emotional check-in, plan couple time, and remain flexible.

Affirmation: "In our partnership, we are stronger together. Our love multiplies our individual strengths. We prioritize our relationship and treat each other with compassion."

Career Confidence: Thriving as a Professional

Queens, let me say this – your career is not just a job. It's a platform for your brilliance to shine. As women, we often have to work twice as hard to get half as far. But guess what? We do it with grace, style, and unshakeable confidence.

I remember walking into boardrooms where I was the only woman, let alone the only Black woman. But I didn't shrink. I stood tall, knowing that my presence was not just for me but for every sister coming up behind me.

To excel in my career while managing my roles as a wife and mother, I prioritize setting clear work boundaries. This helps me stay focused and productive during work hours, without feeling guilty about my other responsibilities. I implement this by sticking to defined work hours, minimizing distractions, transitioning out of work mode, and practicing self-compassion.

This strategy keeps me confident and effective at work, while also protecting time for my family and personal well-being.

Affirmation: "My voice is powerful, my ideas are valuable, and my presence is necessary. I prioritize my career goals with intention and treat myself with compassion as I grow."

Professional Success: Managing a University-Wide Event

As an executive administrative assistant to university leaders, I was tasked with organizing a high-stakes university-wide event that involved coordinating multiple departments, managing logistics, and ensuring the attendance of key stakeholders. This event was crucial for the university's public image and relationship-building efforts, so the pressure was high.

Intentional Prioritization

With so many moving parts, I knew I couldn't manage everything at once. To handle the challenge, I focused on intentional prioritization by identifying key tasks, delegating where possible, and communicating clearly with leadership.

Self-Compassion in the Process

The pressure to make the event perfect was intense, and there were moments when I felt overwhelmed. Practicing self-compassion became essential by accepting imperfection, taking breaks, and acknowledging effort.

Challenges Overcome

One major challenge was a last-minute change in the speaker schedule, which could have caused chaos for the event flow. Instead of panicking, I adjusted the timeline, communicated with the speaker team, and calmly worked out a solution without letting it derail the entire event. This moment of crisis was managed because I prioritized communication and adaptability, all while staying composed under pressure.

Outcome

The event was a success—leadership was pleased, and the feedback from attendees was overwhelmingly positive. The intentional prioritization I employed allowed me to navigate the complexities of the event, and my practice of self-compassion kept me grounded and focused throughout the process.

Motherhood: Nurturing, Balancing, and Thriving

Now, let's talk about one of the most challenging and rewarding roles – motherhood. It's a 24/7 job that doesn't come with a manual, but it does come with endless love and countless teachable moments.

Motherhood for us is about more than just raising children; it's about raising future leaders, thinkers, and change-makers. It's about instilling in them the strength and resilience that runs through our veins.

Motherhood Moment: Navigating a Child's Illness

A transformative moment in my motherhood journey occurred when my five-year-old fell seriously ill. As I managed frequent doctor visits and constant care while being four months pregnant and working full-time, I had to reevaluate my priorities.

Intentional Prioritization:

With so many demands on my time, I realized I couldn't do everything. My primary focus had to be on the well-being of both my children, ensuring they received the attention they needed.

Focusing on Health and Emotional Support:

I prioritized my child's immediate needs—attending appointments and providing emotional support. I accepted that household tasks could wait; my children's recovery was what mattered most.

Simplifying My Workload:

At work, I communicated openly about my situation and delegated tasks. Seeking flexibility helped me manage my workload without feeling overwhelmed, emphasizing the importance of asking for help.

Self-Compassion in the Process:

During this challenging time, I practiced self-compassion by taking time for myself and being gentle with myself.

How This Experience Shaped My Approach to Motherhood

This experience taught me that intentional prioritization involves making choices that reflect what truly matters. I focus on being present with my children, recognizing that some days are about connection rather than productivity.

I also learned the value of self-compassion. Embracing imperfection has made me a more patient mother, and I now prioritize self-care, understanding that I can't pour from an empty cup. Ultimately, I realized that prioritizing what matters while giving myself grace is essential in both motherhood and life.

Affirmation: "I am nurturing the future. My love and guidance are shaping lives and legacies. I prioritize my children's needs while also honoring my own."

Self-Care Superpowers: The Key to Being a Wonder Woman

Lean in because this is crucial: You cannot share from an empty vessel. Self-care isn't selfish; it's necessary. It's the fuel that keeps your wonder woman powers charged.

I had to learn this lesson the hard way. I was giving, giving, giving until I had nothing left. That's when I realized that taking care of myself wasn't a luxury; it was a necessity.

Incorporating Intentional Self-Care

Understanding the vital role of self-care in my busy life, I incorporated practices such as prayer, journaling, stretching, walks, and dancing into my daily routine. Each of these elements played a unique role in enhancing my well-being. Additionally, seeking counseling boosted my self-awareness, enabling me to practice self-compassion and strengthen my relationships with family and colleagues.

Integrating these practices resulted in profound changes, significantly reducing my stress and anxiety, enhancing my physical well-being, boosting my mood and resilience, and fostering a deeper connection with myself.

Affirmation: "I prioritize my well-being because I deserve care and compassion, especially from myself. My self-care is non-negotiable."

Self-Care Strategy: Daily Gratitude Journaling

I practice daily gratitude journaling, taking just five minutes each evening to note three things I'm thankful for that day. This simple ritual allows me to focus on the positive aspects of my life, even during challenging times. I maintain this practice by setting a consistent time, keeping my journal easily accessible, allowing for flexibility, and reflecting on my progress.

This strategy not only enhances my overall well-being but also fosters a more positive outlook, helping me navigate my roles with gratitude and grace.

Call to Action

Now, it's your turn, sis. I want you to take out a piece of paper right now. Yes, right now. Write down three things:

1. One area of your life where you need to practice more intentional prioritization.
2. One self-compassionate act you're going to commit to this week.
3. One strategy from this chapter that you're going to implement starting today.

Personal Reflection: The Journey of Balancing Multiple Roles

Navigating the roles of wife, mother, and career professional has taught me that intentional prioritization and self-compassion are essential. Early in my journey, I often felt overwhelmed, trying to juggle every responsibility perfectly. I wish I had known sooner that prioritization means focusing on what truly matters—quality time with my children, meaningful work, and nurturing my relationship with my partner.

Self-Compassion:

I also wish I had embraced self-compassion earlier. Holding myself to impossibly high standards only led to exhaustion. Acknowledging my limitations and allowing myself grace has been transformative, reminding me that my worth isn't defined by productivity.

By prioritizing intentionally and practicing self-compassion, I've found greater balance and fulfillment. While my journey continues, I hope to inspire others to approach their roles with kindness, knowing it's about creating a life aligned with true values, not perfection.

Listen, this journey isn't about perfection. It's about progress. It's about intentionally creating a life that honors all parts of you – the wife, the worker, and the wonder woman.

You have the power to rewrite your story. To create a life of purpose, balance, and joy. It won't be easy, but I promise you, it will be worth it.

As we close this chapter, take note: You are not just balancing roles; you're orchestrating a beautiful, complex life. You're not just surviving; you're thriving. And with every challenge you overcome, every boundary you set, and every act of love you put into motion, you're not just changing your life – you're changing the world.

The key is intentional prioritization and self-compassion. Choose what matters most in each moment, and be kind to yourself along the way. You're doing amazing, sis.

In the next chapter, we'll explore how to take this balancing act to the next level, creating a support system that extends beyond our immediate family and into our community. We'll talk about building and nurturing the village that it takes to not just raise a child, but to uplift a generation.

Now, go forth and conquer, my beautiful, balanced, bold sister. The world is waiting for the magic only you can bring.

Verna Lee Burney

INTRINSIC HAPPINESS

Embracing Resilience in the Face of Adversity

15

INTRINSIC HAPPINESS

EMBRACING RESILIENCE IN THE FACE OF ADVERSITY

By: Verna Lee Burney

To create a safe environment both physically and emotionally in order to thrive. Creating a safe space, both physically and emotionally, is essential for healing and thriving after trauma. With faith, resilience, and the courage to rest and rise again, we can find strength in our vulnerability. Through professional support and self-compassion, we are guided by God's grace, finding victory in our journey toward wholeness and personal growth.

The Power of Resilience and Intrinsic Happiness

In the quiet corners of our souls, where dreams whisper and hope takes root, there lies a wellspring of strength waiting to be tapped. Dear sister, as you stand at the crossroads of transformation, know that within you burns an eternal flame—the resilient bloom of intrinsic happiness.

Our journey begins with a profound truth: creating a safe environment, both physically and emotionally, is not just a luxury—it's a necessity for healing and thriving. As we navigate the landscape of our experiences, remember that your vulnerability is not a weakness, but a gateway to immense strength.

With each step you take, with each challenge you face, you are cultivating a space of safety and growth. Your faith, your resilience, and your courage to both rest and rise again are the cornerstones of your journey. In this sacred space, guided by God's grace, you will find the victory that awaits in your path toward wholeness and personal growth.

This chapter is your compass, guiding you from the shadows of helplessness to the radiant light of hopefulness. Let us embark on a journey to craft a new story, one where you are the heroine of your own empowering saga.

Ground Zero - The Foundation of Rebirth

At Ground Zero, where the dust of shattered expectations settles, we find the fertile soil of new beginnings. Here, in this sacred space of renewal, your story of resilience takes flight.

Remember, dear one, that in the face of life's storms, you have a choice. Will you allow the winds of adversity to break you, or will you bend like the willow, gathering strength in your flexibility? As Maya Angelou once said, "You may encounter many defeats, but you must not be defeated."

Ground Zero is not your ending; it is the prologue to your renaissance. Here, we plant the seeds of intrinsic happiness, watered by the tears of your past and nourished by the sunlight of your potential.

Rise and Shine - Summoning Your Inner Luminosity

As the phoenix rises from the ashes, so too shall you emerge, radiant and renewed. It's time to rise and shine, to let your inner light pierce through the veil of doubt.

> Happiness is an art,
> We must guide it with the genuineness of our hearts.
> Happiness should come from within,
> Our happiness should not be
> determined by how often a person grins.

In the masterpiece of your life, you are both the artist and the canvas. Each challenge you face is a chance to add vibrant hues to your story. Remember, the brightest rainbows often follow the darkest storms.

Embracing Resilience in the Face of Adversity

Resilience, my sister, is not the absence of struggle but the courage to continue in spite of it. It's the unwavering belief that you are more than your circumstances, more than the sum of your trials.

The base of happiness must be resolved in our hearts from within. This allows us to see and be in adversity and still choose to grin as we win.

As a woman of color navigating the complexities of life, you carry the strength of your ancestors in your DNA. Their resilience flows through your veins, a testament to the power of perseverance in the face of adversity.

Unlocking Your Power - The Journey from Self-Doubt to Self-Sovereignty

Now, let us unlock the vault of your inner power. It's time to shed the cloak of self-doubt and step into the light of self-sovereignty.

> The winner from within speaks testament
> of a faith that is solid and locked in,
> The reason a person is able to
> continue to grin and win,
> Someone's consciousness decided to
> Let it be resolved from within.

Your voice matters. Your dreams are valid. Your worth is immeasurable. As Audre Lorde reminds us, "When I dare to be powerful, to use my strength in the service of my vision, then it becomes less and less important whether I am afraid."

Nurturing the Seeds of Self-Belief - Cultivating Your Garden of Possibility

In the garden of your soul, tend to the seeds of self-belief with the care of a master gardener. Water them with affirmations, nourish them with knowledge, and let them bask in the sunlight of your unwavering faith.

> A choice was made to defy all adversity
> and cling to their intrinsic happiness from within.
> Happiness from within has the power to
> charge the brain with a sense of electricity,
> That alludes to an attitude that I always win.

Remember, you are not just growing a garden; you are cultivating an Eden of endless possibilities. Your dreams are the flowers that will bloom in this paradise of your making.

The Eternal Flame of Intrinsic Happiness

As we close this chapter, know that the journey to intrinsic happiness is ongoing. It's a path illuminated by the light of your resilience, paved with the stones of your determination.

You, my dear sister, are a beacon of hope. Your story of transformation will inspire others to rise, to shine, to claim their own happiness from within.

As we step forward into the realm of "Embracing Change and Flexibility," remember that your ability to adapt is your superpower. The winds of change may blow, but you are the captain of your ship, steering towards the shores of your dreams with unwavering resolve.

In the words of Toni Morrison, "You are your best thing." Embrace this truth, and let it guide you as we navigate the ever-changing tides of life in our next chapter.

Monica Alexander

BREAKING BOUNDARIES

From Expectation to Empowerment

16

BREAKING BOUNDARIES

FROM EXPECTATION TO EMPOWERMENT
By: Monica Alexander

Monica Alexander is a former telecom executive specializing in technology and customer experience who empowers women to break through barriers in both corporate and personal spheres. Drawing from her journey in digital transformation and AI leadership, she guides others in transforming challenges into opportunities for growth.

As immediate past president of WICT-Carolinas and NAMIC-Carolinas, co-founder of Synergy Better Together Marriage Ministry, and active member of both Alpha Kappa Alpha Sorority, Inc. and The Links, Inc., Monica demonstrates how authentic leadership creates lasting impact across all dimensions of life.

Connect with Monica at https://synergybettertogether.com

Reclaiming Your Life and Living on Purpose

Life is a journey packed with experiences and dreams. At some point, we all face moments when change shows up, offering a chance to discover strength we never knew we had.

This chapter walks with you through that transformation, grounded in the promise of Isaiah 54:17 (KJV): "No weapon that is formed against thee shall prosper; and every tongue that shall rise against thee in judgment thou shalt condemn."

As a woman of color navigating the complex landscapes of personal and professional life, I've learned that this verse isn't just comforting—it's a call to action. It's an invitation to see our struggles through a new lens, to transform our difficulties into strength, and to live a life that aligns with our deepest purpose.

The Expectation Trap: Unmasking the Lies

I sat, eyes glued to the screen, watching the presidential debate unfold. The initial handshake, 45's averted gaze when facing Vice President Kamala Harris, the subsequent news cycle spinning "We still don't know her"...

Each moment felt like a punch to the gut, stirring up memories and emotions I thought I'd left behind.

As I watched, I found myself mentally flipping through a catalog of my own experiences as a woman of color.

Times when I was overlooked, underestimated, or expected to conform to someone else's idea of who I should be. How many of us have felt this way?

Trapped by expectations that have nothing to do with our true worth or capabilities?

These expectations, these lies, they whisper:

1. Women, especially women of color, must constantly prove themselves.
2. Avoidance or dismissal diminishes our worth or capability.
3. If we're not known in a certain way, we're not qualified or valuable.

Cultural expectations further bind us:

1. Women/girls should be seen and not heard.
2. Respect your elders and authority without question.
3. Work hard and your work will speak for itself.
4. Be a strong black woman—a fixer like Olivia Pope.

But here's the truth: You are not defined by these expectations. You are not the sum of others' projections and biases.

You're not just a job title, a relationship status, or a number on a scale. You're a beating heart, a queen, a force of nature waiting to be unleashed.

Remember, as Isaiah 54:17 reminds us, others' judgments don't have the final say. Our worth isn't determined by meeting societal expectations, but by our identity in Christ.

Take a moment. Breathe deep. Now say to yourself these words of affirmation: "I am more than society's expectations. I am God's masterpiece in progress, constantly evolving and growing."

Reflection Question: What expectations or judgments have you internalized that contradict God's view of you? How can you begin to replace these with God's truths?

When Life is Life'ing: Resilience or Surrender?

Life has a way of continually presenting us with moments that test our resolve and sense of self-worth. As a woman of color in the field of technology, I've faced my share of these tests. There were countless times when I was the only woman, often the only person of color, at the table.

1. First grade in Detroit, hiding your southern accent.
2. Being 1 of 5 women of color in your college program studying Management Information Systems in the mid-90's.
3. The pivotal moment in September 2019, deciding whether to enter the Future Leaders Program, leave my team for a potential opportunity to become a Vice President.

In each of these moments, I was faced with 'weapons' formed against me - stereotypes, isolation, self-doubt. But I began to understand that these weapons would only succeed if I allowed them to.

Using the power of self-reflection, I realized that to truly overcome these challenges, I needed to look inward. As the Serenity Prayer teaches us, I needed the wisdom to know what I could change and what I couldn't.

I also had to adopt the truth that if I couldn't be honest with myself about how I was feeling, I'd struggle to be honest with others.

Through these experiences, I learned that resilience isn't about never facing challenges. It's about facing them head-on, being honest with yourself, and choosing to grow through them rather than be diminished by them.

Remember this: your ancestors didn't just survive; they thrived. That same strength runs through your veins. When life comes at you hard, stand firm. Your resilience is your superpower.

Reflection Question: What 'weapons' are you facing right now? How can you apply the wisdom of Isaiah 54:17 and the Serenity Prayer to your situation?

Breaking the Chains: From Captive to Conqueror

It's time to break those chains. Yes, the ones that say you're not enough, that you don't belong, that you can't achieve your dreams. Those chains? They're nothing but lies.

Let me say it a different way, now is the time to break the chains of self-doubt and limitations! Well, how? Glad that you asked. Remember the uncomfortable moments we discussed - the presidential debate stirring up memories, the challenges of being the only woman of color in the room? These experiences, once seeming like weapons against us, can become tools God uses to shape us into conquerors.

Romans 8:28 reminds us, "And we know that in all things God works for the good of those who love him, who have been called according to his purpose." This isn't just spiritual comfort food - it's an invitation to see our struggles through a new lens.

Through my journey - from hiding my southern twang in Detroit to leaping into the Future Leaders Program - I learned the power of embracing discomfort. Like a weight lifter building strength through resistance, or precious metal refined by fire, I grew stronger through challenges.

I realized my true strength lay in vulnerability and faith. What once seemed like obstacles - my accent, gender, background - became unique qualities diversifying every room I entered.

The Power of Perspective became crucial. Life's seasons, like nature's, work together to shape our journey. Just as Fall feels different in

Florida versus New York City, our challenges and triumphs are experienced differently based on our perspective.

Understanding this principle helped me view my "seasons" of struggle not as setbacks, but as opportunities for growth. Whether in a Winter of challenge preparing for a Spring of opportunity, or a Summer of success readying for future transitions, the key is recognizing your season and applying the proper context.

By shifting our perspective, we transform challenges from weapons against us into tools God uses to shape us. This mindset breaks the chains of negativity, allowing us to step into God's purpose, regardless of our current season.

The Resilience Arsenal: Real Strategies for Real Life

Now, let's talk strategy. Because dreaming is beautiful, but doing? That's where the magic happens. As conquerors and rising queens, we need practical tools to turn our empowered mindset into action. Let's build a resilience arsenal that transforms our challenges into stepping stones:

1. **Establish Your Resilience Routine:** Create a daily practice that strengthens your spirit. This could include devotion, journaling, meditation, exercise, or any form of consistent self-care that prepares you to reign over your day.
2. **Champion Your Journey:** Start a Champion's Journal. Document your victories, both big and small. Record the challenges you've conquered, the risks you've taken, and the unexpected doors God has opened. This practice reveals how every step contributes to your rising.
3. **Embrace Progress Over Perfection:** Like the river persistently flowing over rocks, resilience isn't about avoiding obsta-

cles but consistently moving forward, gradually carving your unique path.
4. **Practice Patience and Grace:** Remember, it's like mastering your grandmother's cornbread dressing recipe. Developing resilience takes time. Give yourself the grace to grow and improve with each attempt.

Remember Audre Lorde's powerful words: "Caring for myself is not self-indulgence, it is self-preservation, and that is an act of political warfare." In your journey, self-care is not just personal—it's revolutionary.

Lesson learned: Resilience is a skill that can be developed and strengthened over time.

Reflection question: What tools can you add to your personal 'resilience arsenal' this week?

Living Unleashed: Your Life, God's Design

You were created for a purpose. Not to shrink, not to blend in, but to shine.

Now that we've built our resilience arsenal, it's time to live unleashed - to fully embrace God's design for our lives.

"Our deepest fear is not that we are inadequate. Our deepest fear is that we are powerful beyond measure." - Marianne Williamson

Living unleashed means embracing all of who you are, using your gifts, and walking in your purpose. It's not always easy, but it's always worth it.

A personal experience taught me the power of being open to unexpected opportunities. When a friend couldn't make a graduation speech, she connected me with the organizer. This simple introduction led to attending an event where I discovered an opportunity to live out my purpose - motivating and inspiring others.

Technology was my comfort zone, but public speaking and leadership development were not. Yet, taking that one small step led to an exciting, unexpected path. The lesson? Don't get too tied to what you think your next step should be. Be open and nurture authentic relationships.

Remember, you were created for a purpose. Romans 12:2 tells us, "Do not conform to the pattern of this world, but be transformed by the renewing of your mind."

1 Corinthians 12 reminds us that we're all unique parts of one body. Don't compare yourself to others - each of us has a unique purpose.

To live unleashed, align yourself with who God says you are:

- Created in His image
- Blessed and highly favored
- More than a conqueror
- The head and not the tail

These aren't just sayings – they're truths about your identity. Embrace them and see yourself through God's eyes.

Embracing your purpose often means stepping out of your comfort zone and believing in who God says you are, not succumbing to the world's expectations or biases.

Reflection: How can you start living 'unleashed' in alignment with God's design for your life?

Call to Action:

1. Challenge one: limiting expectation this week.

2. Start a daily gratitude practice.
3. Set a bold goal and take one step towards it today.
4. Encourage someone who needs strength.
5. Create a vision board representing your unleashed life.

"Every time you state what you want or believe, you're the first to hear it. It's a message to both you and others about what you think is possible." - Oprah Winfrey

Your determination is unstoppable. It's the force that turns dreams into reality and creates legacies.

Affirmation: "I am resilient. I am powerful. I am unstoppable."

As we stand at the edge of greatness, let us step into the embrace of independence, our hearts filled with courage, our paths lit by the glow of confidence. This is not the end, but the beginning of a story that will be told for generations—a story of the Savvy Single Sister: Celebrating Independence with Courage and Confidence.

Remember, you are more than a conqueror. You are a visionary, breaking boundaries and redefining what it means to live on purpose. As you step into this new chapter of your life, carry with you the wisdom of your experiences, the strength of your resilience, and the assurance that no weapon formed against you shall prosper. Your journey is just beginning, and the world is waiting for the unique gift that only you can bring.

Thelesa Moore

SAVVY SINGLE SISTER

Celebrating Independence with Courage and Confidence

17

SAVVY SINGLE SISTER

CELEBRATING INDEPENDENCE
WITH COURAGE AND CONFIDENCE

By Thelesa Moore

Thelesa Moore is CEO of Elevate Up 365 and author of "The Flight of Your Life: A Guide to Overcoming Domestic Abuse." She empowers women to evolve into leaders and excel in every aspect of their lives. Her chapter in "Girl, There's a Champion in You," Single Savvy Sister embraces the season of singleness.

Her story connects with like-minded women. The audience will be captivated by her resilience. Thelesa's passion is helping women become a better version of themselves. You will reap the harvest if you don't give up. Connect with Thelesa @Moore.Thelesa on Facebook.com and Thelesa@elevateup365.com

Let us not be weary in doing good, for at the proper time we will reap a harvest if we don't give up. (Galatians 6:9-10 NIV)

Trust in the Lord with all your heart and lean not to your own understanding; in all your ways submit to him, and he will make your paths straight. (Proverbs 3:5-6 NIV)

The Symphony of Self-Reliance

Listen up, beautiful Black queen! This is your anthem, your call to arms, your declaration of independence. We're about to embark on a journey that'll shake you to your core and lift you higher than you've ever been.

This chapter is for every single, straight, Black woman out there who's been carrying the weight of the world on her shoulders, feeling overworked, lonely, and misunderstood.

But before we dive in, let's anchor ourselves in a truth that's as old as time and as fresh as tomorrow's sunrise. Remember this: "Let us not be weary in doing good, for at the proper time we will reap a harvest if we don't give up." Your journey, sister, is not in vain.

Every step you take, every challenge you face, is planting seeds for a future harvest beyond your wildest dreams.

And when the road gets tough, when you're tempted to lean on your own understanding, that's when you need to "Trust in the Lord with all your heart." Submit your ways to Him, and watch as He straightens your path, guiding you towards a destiny that's uniquely yours.

Now, with these principles lighting our way, let's turn up the volume on your life and let the world hear your roar! Remember this: You are not alone. You are not incomplete. You are a force of nature, a symphony of strength, resilience, and untapped potential.

Embrace Single Season - Own Your Life

Baby girl, it's time to stop apologizing for your singlehood and start celebrating it! This is your season to shine, to explore, to grow without compromise. You've been told that you're missing something, that you're not whole without a partner. But let me tell you something – that's a lie as old as time, and it's high time we buried it.

If no one else celebrates you, celebrate yourself. Every year when my birthday would come I would go into a depressed state. I mean a sobbing cry filled with emotions. Another year and not married. Then I woke up and said I am going to start celebrating my life.

I made a promise to myself every year for my birthday I choose to go to a different city or place to celebrate. My sister's friends would start asking early, "Where are we going for your birthday?" They would request their time off early. We have had some fun trips. Most of the time it would just be my Mom and I.

Your independence isn't a burden; it's a blessing. It's the freedom to paint your life in the colors of your choosing, to dance to your own rhythm, to build a legacy that's uniquely yours. So when the world tries to dim your light with its expectations, you stand tall and say, "Watch me glow!"

Remember the words of Angela Davis: "I am no longer accepting the things I cannot change. I am changing the things I cannot accept." That's your new mantra, sister. You're not waiting for life to happen to you; you're making it happen on your terms.

Invest in You - Nourish Your Soul

Now, let's talk about investing in your most valuable asset – YOU. This isn't about being selfish; it's about being smart. You've been pouring from an empty cup for too long, and it's time to fill it up to overflowing. My Sunday school teacher would always say, is your cup running over? If it was not running over that meant I only had enough for me. We want to live the life that overflows with abundance.

Your mind is hungry for knowledge, so feed it! Dive into books that challenge and inspire you. Michelle Obama's "Becoming" isn't just a read; it's a revolution waiting to happen between those pages. "Woman to Woman" by Joyce Meyer speaks to the heart about life lessons.

Work on you. I decided I would start being faithful in my workout. I needed a push to get me on the right path. I signed up for a personal trainer. This dude was so hard on me he was a no excuse guy. This man had me running, sweating, pumping iron, squatting.

Somedays I would be on the treadmill crying. I wanted to give up on day one. He would say, "I know you are mad at me. You will appreciate me later." We would work out as a group. Let me tell you. This guy was so bulked and muscular. I did not care about that. At the end of each workout, the only thing I could do was roll over on the floor. I never knew I had it in me.

I never would have pushed myself like that on my own. I have great respect for that man. People would be in the gym cheering me on. They knew I was struggling and wanted to quit. See, we all need encouragement. We became like family. I survived. I can laugh about it now. Everyday I am a work in progress.

Your body is a temple, so treat it like one. Move it, nourish it, rest it. Your spirit needs tending too. Whether it's through prayer, meditation, or simply sitting in silence, give yourself the space to connect with God.

And let's not forget about your finances, queen. It's time to get that money right! Educate yourself on investment, savings, and building generational wealth. Your financial independence is your ticket to true freedom. Lydia in the Bible was a businesswoman. She sold purple cloth.

Courageous and Confident - Unbreakable Spirit

Walking through this world as a single, Black woman takes courage. It takes confidence. And baby, you've got both in spades – even if you don't always feel it.

Your confidence isn't about being fearless; it's about being brave enough to face your fears and keep moving forward. It's about walking into a room full of doubters and owning every inch of your space.

Put your head up and walk in your purpose. Go for what's yours. Know that you are more than enough. You are the child of the King. Some things we have to do them scared until we build our confidence. Look in that mirror and own it. I may not have it all like Oprah, but I got it. There is no need to compare yourself to anyone. Be the best version of you. You may even have to take a break from social media. Remember, social media is not always the real deal.

Remember, your worth isn't determined by your relationship status or anyone else's opinion of you. It's determined by you and you alone. So stand tall, speak your truth, and let your light shine so bright it blinds the haters.

As Queen Latifah said, "I'm not a woman who follows the crowd. I'm a woman who stands out from the crowd." That's you, sister. Unique, whole, and absolutely unstoppable.

Business Savvy - Making Power Moves

It's time to talk business, because you're not just building a life – you're building an empire. Whether you're climbing the corporate ladder or blazing your own entrepreneurial trail, you've got what it takes to succeed.

Your career isn't just about making money; it's about making an impact. It's about breaking down barriers and opening doors for the sisters coming up behind you.

When I decided to buy a house, that was one hard decision. Everyone was saying you should wait until you are married to buy your house. It was very stressful. I was questioning and second-guessing myself, listening to other people. My Daddy said, "Buy the house. Your husband can always get you something bigger and better." This was an investment. It's cozy and comfortable. I had major headaches going back and forth, trying to decide if I was making the right decision. God provides, I have never been without. I trust God with my Finances. Give that tithe, it will come back to you in more ways than one.

Watch your spending and don't try to live like the Joneses. Start a business. I don't care if you sell cookies and candy. Find something you can do with low startup costs to bring in some extra income. While you are reading my chapter, write a book. You can do it.

Single ladies, you have a lot to bring to the table. I am not coming empty-handed to the table. Secure your bag. Stop paying all that money to carry someone else's name on your shoulder and no money inside your bag. Let's keep it real. Hair done, nails done, makeup done, and you broke as a joke. This has got to stop. It's time to come up, sister. No one else is going to do it for you.

Remember, in the words of Shirley Chisholm, "If they don't give you a seat at the table, bring a folding chair." You're not waiting for opportunities; you're creating them. You're not asking for permission; you're making announcements.

Your business acumen is your superpower. Use it to negotiate better deals, to demand what you're worth, to build the career of your dreams. The boardroom, the startup world, the corner office – they're all waiting for you to make your mark.

Relationships - Attracting Your Tribe

Now, let's get real about relationships. Being single doesn't mean being alone. It means having the freedom to cultivate connections that truly serve you.

You are what you attract, so be intentional about the energy you put out into the world. Surround yourself with people who celebrate your independence, who push you to grow, who show up for you in both sunshine and storm.

Ladies, I get it that we all want that special one. Maybe Ken has not found you yet. You know Ken from when we were little girls playing house. We would play with our dolls, like we were the Mama, and Ken would be the Daddy, and off to work he would go. You know the picture that was painted for us as a child. Girl, nobody told me Ken would be so long coming home.

Sometimes we get impatient when Ken does not come home. We start to settle. I settled, you talk about a hot mess. Yes I experienced some horrible relationships. One that had physical and verbal abuse. It is not worth it. I have zero tolerance for that behavior.

Do not start saying you don't need a man. Honey, you need a man, just like they need us. What do I mean by that? You need a good mechanic, plumber, and yard crew because I am not cutting the grass. I don't like being in the sun like that.

Sometimes I just need help putting the light bulbs in high ceilings. Now, granted all of these men are hired help until I have my own that does it all. That's what I work for: to get the things I want. Saves me time and effort.

Keep a good support group. I have good friends I can call on, laugh with, and cry with. Toss out ideas. I also have places that I volunteer for that help strengthen my mental health and overall well-being while using my creativity. My volunteer work is my calling. My career is what I get paid for. There is a difference.

Your tribe isn't limited to romantic partners. It's your girlfriends who hold you down, your mentors who lift you up, and your family (blood or chosen) who love you unconditionally.

These are the relationships that will sustain you, challenge you, and help you become the best version of yourself.

And when it comes to romance? Don't settle. Wait for someone who adds to your life, who respects your independence, who sees your strength as sexy. You're not looking for someone to complete you – you're already whole. You're looking for someone to complement the masterpiece that is you.

Your Unfolding Story

Beautiful, brave, brilliant sister – this is just the beginning of your story. You're writing a narrative of independence, courage, and unshakeable confidence with every choice you make, every challenge you overcome, every goal you crush.

Remember, your single season isn't a waiting room for the next chapter of your life. It is the chapter – rich, full, and brimming with possibility. Embrace it. Celebrate it. Live it to the fullest.

As you step into your power, know that you're not just changing your own life – you're changing the world. You're redefining what it means to be a single, Black woman in this society. You're showing the next generation what's possible when you believe in yourself and refuse to be limited by anyone else's expectations.

So go forth and conquer, my savvy single sister. Your time is now. Your moment is here. The world is waiting for the gift that only you can give. Shine on!

As we close this chapter of self-discovery and empowerment, we turn our gaze to the horizon where new challenges and triumphs await. In our next exploration, we'll dive into "The Champion's Journey: Embracing Your Power and Changing the World." Get ready to take your hard-earned wisdom and newfound confidence and use them to make waves in ways you've never imagined!

Mary H. Davis

THE FINAL ROUND

The Next Champion Rises
"Fight For it"

18

THE FINAL ROUND

THE NEXT CHAMPION RISES

"FIGHT FOR IT"

By Mary H. Davis

> "They thought the glass ceiling would hold us back. Watch it shatter under our championship punches. I'm not here to participate—I'm here to devastate the whole damn system."
> – Mary H. Davis

THE FINAL ROUND: NO MORE WAITING

Forget gentle beginnings. We're here to demolish limitations. Like heavyweight champions who don't just win fights—we reconstruct the entire boxing world. Each punch we throw crashes through decades of "you can't," each combination demolishes generations of "not yet."

Look in that mirror, Champion. You see what they see? They see a contender. BUT YOU? You'd better see an unstoppable force that's about to set this whole game on fire.

No more waiting for the bell. No more polite touch of gloves. It's time to TAKE what's yours.

We've ALWAYS Been The Blueprint –

Now We're Taking The Whole Damn Arena

For too long, they've watched Black women build empires with our bare hands—creating wealth for everyone but ourselves. Think we're just now learning to fight? We invented the game they're playing.

The Raw Numbers That End TODAY:

- 63 cents to their dollar? We're not closing gaps—we're creating new economies
- Less than 1% of Venture Capital funding? Watch us build billion-dollar empires from their breadcrumbs
- The wealth gap? We're not bridging it—we're leaping over it and building our own banks

This Isn't Just A Fight – It's A TAKEOVER

Forget asking for seats at tables. We're flipping tables and building skyscrapers. You think pay equity is the goal? That's just our warm-up round.

CHAMPION MOVES:

- **DOMINATE,** Don't Just Deliver – Your excellence isn't a request, it's a hostile takeover
- **NEGOTIATE** Like You Own The Arena – Because after this round, you will

- **BUILD** Empires On Their Excuses – Every "no" funds your next acquisition

We're not here for equality—we're here for TOTAL ECONOMIC DOMINATION. When one of us breaks through, we're bringing the whole dynasty with us.

The Champion's INNERMOST CIRCLE – Build Your UNSTOPPABLE Force

This is why I love boxing. Champions don't just train—they cultivate GREATNESS. Every person in your corner better be ready for war because we're not just winning rounds—we're changing the whole sport.

Your Elite Squad:

- The **VISION MASTER** – Sees victory before the bell rings
- The **DOOR DEMOLISHER** – Doesn't knock politely—KICKS walls down
- The **EMPIRE BUILDER** – Turns your influence into institutions
- The **STANDARD DESTROYER** – Shatters "good enough" on sight
- The **LEGACY MAKER** – Turns your blueprint into their launching pad

RIGHT NOW: Check your corner. Anyone not adding fire to your fury needs to GO.

Your circle isn't just support—it's your ammunition. Build a team that makes excellence look BASIC.

Creating DYNASTIES –

The Ownership REVOLUTION

Miss me with that corporate ladder talk—we're building ROCKET SHIPS. Ownership isn't a goal—it's the MINIMUM. We're not just buying buildings; we're reconstructing skylines.

The Champion's ARSENAL:

- **Knowledge?** We're WEAPONIZING our expertise into DIGITAL EMPIRES
- **Experience?** We're packaging it into PREMIUM PRODUCTS
- **Wisdom?** We're monetizing it through GLOBAL PLATFORMS

EXECUTE WITH FORCE:

- Turn Your Expertise into **PASSIVE INCOME MACHINES**
- Package Your Solutions into **SCALABLE PRODUCTS** that sell while you sleep
- Transform Your Knowledge into **DIGITAL ASSETS** that build generational wealth
- Leverage Technology to take **LOCAL** wisdom into **GLOBAL** dominance

This isn't just about sharing what you know—it's about TURNING YOUR MIND into a MULTI-MILLION DOLLAR ENTERPRISE. In this economy, your intellectual property isn't just valuable—it's REVOLUTIONARY CURRENCY.

The Final Round - UNLEASH YOUR REIGN

The most dangerous champion isn't the one who hits hardest—it's the one who REFUSES TO STAY DOWN. This isn't just your round; it's your TAKEOVER SEASON.

You're Not Just Fighting For Victory; You're Fighting For:

- **COMPLETE CONTROL** of every table you've been denied
- An **ARMY** of future Black women champions

- A **LEGACY** so powerful it rewrites history

This isn't about breaking records—it's about CREATING NEW CATEGORIES OF GREATNESS.

Champion's COMMANDMENTS:

- **DEMOLISH** Limitations – Your presence is a force of nature
- **REJECT** Doubt – Fear is too expensive for your tax bracket
- **TRANSFORM** Opposition – Every "no" funds your empire

Your Next Move – JOIN THE REVOLUTION

This isn't an ending—it's a DECLARATION OF DOMINANCE.

Enter the Champion's DOMINION! The Girl, There's A Champion in You Community isn't just a network—it's an UNSTOPPABLE FORCE.

Write the Next Chapter of GREATNESS. Become an author in our next volume. Your story isn't motivation—it's a BLUEPRINT FOR DOMINATION.

Join the revolution and claim your crown in the next championship saga.

The Champion's BATTLE CRY

- I DON'T REQUEST POWER—**I SEIZE KINGDOMS**
- I DON'T CHASE OPPORTUNITY—**I CREATE INDUSTRIES**
- I WASN'T BORN TO FIT IN—**I WAS BUILT TO DOMINATE**

History stalls until Black women step into the ring. The next champion isn't approaching—she's HERE, and she's about to show them what unstoppable looks like.

Lace up those gloves. This isn't just your round. This is your REIGN.

And Champion? You were born for total domination.

#WatchMeTAKEOVER

Mary H. Davis - Curator
The Strategist Behind the Knockout

Mary H. Davis doesn't wait to be invited—she builds her own damn ring and dares women to step into theirs.

This isn't your typical "follow your dreams" fairy tale. Mary is a technically trained boxer who threw down her corporate gloves after dominating trillion-dollar companies for decades, walked away from seven-figure potential, and said "enough" to playing small in spaces that were never designed for women like her to win.

She's not just a coach—she's a disruptor, a space-clearer, and the unapologetic fire behind a movement built for women who are tired of shrinking. Mary doesn't do gentle nudges or soft whispers. She's the voice that says, "Stop asking for permission to take up space that's already yours."

As the founder of the Women's Level Up Network, Mary equips women—especially those navigating the intersection of being brilliant, Black, and bold—to demolish their limiting narratives, speak truth to power, and lead like the legacy-builders they were born to be. Her coaching doesn't just change careers; it rewrites bloodlines. Her anthologies don't just publish stories; they birth movements.

Through WLUN, dozens of women have stopped code-switching their power, stopped negotiating their worth, and started showing up as the champions they've always been. They've launched businesses, secured promotions, left toxic relationships, and most importantly, they've remembered who the hell they are.

Girl, There's a Champion in You isn't just a book. It's a battle cry wrapped in a blueprint. It's proof that your story isn't just yours—it's the key someone else has been praying for. And Mary? She's not just the curator. She's the one in your corner, wrapping your gloves, calling out your greatness when you can't see it yourself, and reminding you that it's not just your time—it's your era.

Ready to stop playing defense with your life? Mary's got your back, your front, and every angle in between.

Connect with Mary H. Davis & WLUN

- **Website**: www.womenslevelupnetwork.com
- **Appointment**: www.Appointmentwithwlun.com
- **Facebook**: Women's Level Up Network
- **Instagram**: Women 's_Level_Up_Network
- **LinkedIn**: Women's Level Up Network
- **Email**: Mary@womenslevelupnetwork.com

"Mary created a safe space for me to tell my story for the first time. I didn't even know how much I needed it until I started writing. She challenged me, encouraged me, and reminded me that my voice matters. This wasn't just about becoming a published author—it was about becoming seen."

— Angel Ewings, Co-Author

"Working with Mary through WLUN wasn't just coaching—it was liberation. She helped me see that my corporate experience wasn't something to apologize for, but something to weaponize for good. Now I'm not just surviving in my industry, I'm rewriting the rules."

— Champion Network Member

#WatchUsWork #ChampionRising #WomensLevelUpNetwork

www.ingramcontent.com/pod-product-compliance
Lightning Source LLC
Chambersburg PA
CBHW070055080526
44586CB00013B/1063